BEING
CHRISTIAN

STEPHEN ARTERBURN

AND JOHN SHORE

BEING CHRISTIAN

EXPLORING WHERE
YOU, GOD, AND LIFE
CONNECT

BETHANY HOUSE
PUBLISHERS

Published by Bethany House Publishers
11400 Hampshire Avenue South
Bloomington, Minnesota 55438

Bethany House Publishers is a division of
Baker Publishing Group, Grand Rapids, Michigan.

Printed in the United States of America

ISBN 978-0-7642-0229-2 (International Trade Paper)

The Library of Congress has cataloged the hardcover edition as follows:

Arterburn, Stephen, 1953–
    Being Christian : exploring where you, God, and life connect / Stephen Arterburn and John Shore.
       p.   cm.
    Summary: "A comprehensive introduction and guide to Christianity includes core truths, information, and insights for those new to the Christian faith or curious about it, presented in a combination of narrative chapters and question/answer chapters"— Provided by publisher.
    ISBN 978-0-7642-0426-5 (hardcover : alk. paper) 1. Christianity. I. Shore, John, 1958– II. Title.
    BR121.3.A78   2008
    230—dc22

                                                                        2008028253

To *Sharon Barnes,*

who has shown me, my daughter Madeline,

and all of us who work at New Life

what being Christian looks like.

During good times and bad,

no matter what, just being Christian to those

fortunate enough to know her.

—Steve Arterburn

To *my wife, Catherine,*

who every day shows me what it means to live

with God's love.

—John Shore

He got up and rebuked the wind and said to the sea, "Hush, be still." And the wind died down and it became perfectly calm.

And He said to them, "Why are you afraid? Do you still have no faith?"

They became very much afraid and said to one another, "Who then is this, that even the wind and the sea obey Him?"

—Mark 4:39–41 (NASB)

Contents

Chapter Two: God, You, and Others *67*

Introduction

Are you curious about Christianity? Have you recently become aware of the feeling that God's hand is upon you, that he is ever so gently guiding you toward accepting the truth that some two thousand years ago he really did manifest himself on earth as the man known to history as Jesus Christ? Has something inside been urging you to ignore all that our ever-manic media has been yelling at you about Christianity this week, and to instead find out for yourself what eternal truths Jesus might be waiting to offer you?

If that's where you are, we hope you're excited about what you sense God is saying to you these days.

Or maybe that's not exactly where you are. Maybe you're a little further down the road. Maybe you've already taken a firm hold of the Lord's hand; maybe you've already given yourself to the one whom you know gave himself for you. Maybe, because of your new relationship with him, you're in that thrilling, blessed phase of every believer's life where all you want to do is get to know the Lord better and better every day.

Or, conversely, perhaps you're at the end of a period in your life that began when you started to feel you knew him a little *too* well—when you got bored or restless with God, and as a result sought solace and substance in pastures that at the time seemed greener but turned out to be no fun at all to play in. Perhaps you're just now emerging from the spiritual malaise and/or existential doubt that can sometimes overcome even the most devout of Christ's followers. Maybe now, like the prodigal son himself, you're wanting to return to the arms of the Father, who has never for a moment stopped loving you.

Perhaps none of the above describes you. Perhaps you're someone who has loved the Lord for a long time, who has not wandered away from Jesus, but who's feeling in need of a recharge in your appreciation and enthusiasm for him. Maybe you're just burned out on "religion" and are simply looking to have the fervent immediacy of your love for Jesus rejuvenated.

Wherever you happen to be along the believer's continuum—earnestly curious, recently committed, suddenly saved, lapsed but returning, devoted but seeking reinvigoration—this is the book for you. Because while it's true that different people have different spiritual needs at different times of their lives, everyone always has the same four basic spiritual needs: for *answers*, for *guidance*, for *confirmation*, and for *inspiration*. Here's how we believe this book satisfies all four.

Answers

We asked a lot of people, and did a lot of thinking and praying, in order to come up with the questions about Christianity and its attending issues that we feel even the most experienced believers sometimes want answered. *Being Christian* is not a primer on Christianity; however, it does ask and answer a wide array of the faith's most basic and core questions. Thus you will discover that our response to each inquiry, while always being (if we daresay so ourselves) straightforward and clear, is also informed by all the depth of feeling and thought that the Lord brings to any who believe in, study, and sincerely seek him.

Such questions as "How do I deepen my relationship with God?" and "What if my spouse or family member isn't Christian?" and "How can I increase my compassion for others?" and "How do I keep believing in God after what seems to be a senseless tragedy?" might seem simple—and of course, in their way, they truly are—yet countless books have been written on those and similar other "simple" questions. Here, we demonstrate how the questions and answers we're putting forward are both simple *and* complex. It's our hope that by treating them as such we've succeeded in making of them what we most desire them to be, which are catalysts for a more rewarding understanding and a more direct experiencing of God.

Guidance

Figuring that doing so would pretty thoroughly cover it, we divided this book's questions into two main sections: GOD *Inside,* and GOD *Outside.* The Q and A's found under GOD *Inside* are subdivided into three chapters: "God and You," "God, You, and Others," and "Everyone: Sin, the Human Constant." The Q and A's found under GOD *Outside* fall within two chapters: "The Bible" and "The Church." This structure allows you to locate as quickly as possible (via the Table of Contents) whatever question happens to be most immediately on your mind, and it facilitates the book being readily modified or personalized for the study needs of any individual or group.

Beyond that, we sought to make this book a guide for the enhancement of your relationship with God through two means. First, we made sure the responses to our questions combine two sorts of material: factual and spiritual. It's easy enough to answer questions in a way that satisfies the intellect; we sought to provide answers that at the same time serve to guide you toward the source and substance of all knowledge. Second, we used the questions themselves as a means of spiritual guidance. In this sense, *Being Christian* is most assuredly not *Christianity for Dolts*. "What exactly is the Holy Spirit?" and "Why is repentance so important to me?" are question-types that lend themselves to answers able to illuminate the mind *and* the heart. We sought to provide answers that do both.

Confirmation

It is our belief that at some level of their being everyone who asks a question about Jesus already knows the answer to that question. We believe that the singular challenge of all persons— believers, nonbelievers, doubters, and anyone else anywhere in between—is to strip away everything within them that stands between themselves and their full and (we believe) inevitable love of Jesus. We are certain that people can't help but sense everywhere around and within them the constant, steady, and majestic presence of God.

We believe that in a very real sense, then, people are less interested in knowing what they *don't* know than they are in having definitively confirmed for them what they very strongly *want* to know, which is that God is as real as real gets, and that Jesus Christ was and is God come to earth as a man in order to sacrifice himself as an atonement for their sins. Without in any way shortchanging anyone's intellect or ability to reason, we answered each question with an eye toward affirming the innate knowledge of God we assumed would most likely have been quickened in the soul of anyone asking that question in the first place.

Inspiration

In the final analysis, belief in the reality of God is a dramatic leap from the comfort of the staid, everyday life of our mechanistic world to the blessed free-fall that comes from knowing that God has your back, front, side, top, and everything in between.

Something has to spark one's appreciation of God to go from the theoretical to the actual, from thinking or even hoping that God is real to *knowing* that he is. It is of course our deepest hope that through the power of the Holy Spirit, our words might at some point provide the catalytic flash that transforms one who is seeking into one who has found. And we're confident that if anything we've written here ever does happen to trigger such a magnificent occurrence, it will have as much to do with what we didn't write as with what we did.

We know that you can point someone toward God, but you can never push anyone into a relationship with him. Ultimately, faith is a willful leap, and there's no leap without space between origin and goal. Throughout this book we've endeavored to bear in mind that oftentimes the best way to honor the end result of the greatest leap of all is to honor the integrity of the space it must overcome.

We sincerely hope that through its questions, answers, and the way in which they're organized, *Being Christian* will become for you a means of further understanding and/or discovering your relationship to God. Its purpose is to call you beyond itself; to inspire you to enhance your relationship with God through study, prayer, and reflection; to more freely love and engage both the believers and nonbelievers in your life; to better comprehend and deal with sin; to more regularly and effectively engage God through the glory of his Word; and to help you become an active, informed member of a church in which you feel nurtured, excited, and challenged.

Whoever you are, and wherever you find yourself on the path toward God, we invite you to come with us, as together we move ever closer to the one from whom we all came, and to whom, if we but believe, we will one day gloriously return.

GOD *Inside*

CHAPTER ONE

God and You

Because God, faith, and church can all seem like so much to handle, it's easy to forget that the only thing that really matters is your relationship to God the Father, his son Jesus Christ, and the Holy Spirit. That relationship is the deepest and most personal you'll ever experience. So let's spend some time talking about what it means to say and know you're a Christian.

What's the single most important thing I would have to believe in order to officially qualify as a Christian?

As we're sure you know (but on the very off chance you're not perfectly clear on it), there is no single set of beliefs to which all Christians uniformly agree. There's no regularly updated Register of All Christians kept anywhere, no membership card we're encouraged to laminate and keep with us at all times, no sticker or decal every believer is supposed to stick on his or her car, truck, minivan, or skateboard. There's nothing like that at all.

There's just . . . people, walking around with a lot of different ideas in their minds and hearts. So we want to come alongside you and help you understand what is and isn't true about being Christian.

While many concepts, notions, ideas, and convictions are out there about Christianity, there *are* core beliefs shared by (roughly estimating) 99.99999 percent of all Christians. You'd be extremely hard pressed to find one who doesn't believe, for instance, in the divinity of Jesus Christ. Christians believe that Jesus was both God and man, period. Everything about our faith is grounded in that conviction.

Functionally speaking, one of the great things about Christianity is that it's been around for a very long time. What makes this quality so valuable is its guarantee that such questions as "What do we really believe?" have been thought about, written about, convened about, debated, discussed, refined, and flawlessly articulated for millennia. And throughout history there have been times when, for one reason or another, it was crucial for Christians to be very clear about what exactly it is they believe. The fact that so many minds have given so much attention over so much time to that specific question has resulted in a body of historical documents called creeds (or confessions). Each was formulated in its own time, for its own reason, and to its own effect, but the intent of each was to as fully as possible articulate what Christians believe.

One of the oldest creeds remains of particular importance to Christians around the world today. If you want to know what we believe, you can't go wrong with the Nicene Creed, which is universally acknowledged as a comprehensive and inspired articulation of the faith. Just about everyone who calls themselves Christian will readily claim the Nicene Creed as their own true confession.

The creed is named for the First Council of Nicea, which created its first form. In the fourth century Emperor Constantine called together bishops, leaders, and theologians from all countries to Nicea (in present-day Turkey), for the specific purpose of coming up with a uniform statement of faith that all Christians could agree upon and embrace. Up to that point there'd been certain variations of belief essentially vying for dominance; once the elegant and comprehensive Nicene Creed was issued, it became the standard confession of faith throughout all Christendom. Today millions of Christians around the world—whether Catholic, Orthodox, or Protestant—still include reciting it as part of their regular worship practice.

The Nicene Creed reads as follows:

> *We believe in one God,*
> > *the Father, the Almighty,*
> > *maker of heaven and earth,*
> > *of all that is, seen and unseen.*
>
> *We believe in one Lord, Jesus Christ,*
> > *the only Son of God,*
> > *eternally begotten of the Father,*
> > *God from God, light from light,*
> > *true God from true God,*
> > *begotten, not made,*
> > *of one Being with the Father;*
> > *through him all things were made.*
> > *For us and for our salvation*
> > *he came down from heaven;*
> > *he became incarnate by the Holy Spirit and*
> > > *the virgin Mary,*
> > *and was made man.*
> > *For our sake he was crucified under*
> > > *Pontius Pilate;*
> > *he suffered death and was buried.*
> > *On the third day he rose again*

In accordance with the Scriptures;
he ascended into heaven
and is seated at the right hand of the Father.
He will come again in glory to judge
the living and the dead,
and his kingdom will have no end.

We believe in the Holy Spirit, the Lord, the giver of life,
who proceeds from the Father and the Son,
who with the Father and the Son is
worshiped and glorified,
who has spoken through the prophets.

We believe in one holy catholic [an older word for
"universal"] and apostolic Church.

We acknowledge one baptism for the forgiveness of
sins.

We look for the resurrection of the dead,
and the life of the world to come. Amen.

That is what 99.99999 percent of all Christians have always believed, and what over the centuries countless millions of the faithful have committed to memory.

Other confessions commonly adapted by Protestant denominations are The Apostles' Creed, The Heidelberg Catechism, and The Westminster Confession of Faith.

It's important to note that as inspiring and accessible as they are, Christian confessions are meant to inform and in some way encapsulate Scripture. They are most certainly not, however, meant to replace Scripture.

Fight the good fight of the faith. Take hold of the eternal
life to which you were called when you made your good

confession in the presence of many witnesses. (1 Timothy 6:12)

"The word is near you; it is in your mouth and in your heart," that is, the word of faith we are proclaiming: That if you confess with your mouth, "Jesus is Lord," and believe in your heart that God raised him from the dead, you will be saved. For it is with your heart that you believe and are justified, and it is with your mouth that you confess and are saved. (Romans 10:8–10)

Everyone who confesses Me before men, I will also confess him before My Father who is in heaven. (Matthew 10:32, NASB)

Whoever confesses that Jesus is the Son of God, God abides in him, and he in God. (1 John 4:15, NASB)

Just as we all have criteria for allowing people to come into our home, God has criteria too. We might, for instance, ask that people clean their feet or shoes. Some ask that you take off your shoes. Well, God's requirement of us is Jesus. Through him, now that you've been washed by his sacrifice, you don't come into God's home with just clean feet: you come in with a clean heart too.

Now on to something a bit more mysterious.

What exactly is the Holy Spirit?

The Holy Spirit is God—fully God, not *partially* or *almost* God—and he resides in any believer in Christ. He is the means by which God maintains an immediate, intimate relationship with those who understand his spiritual presence within them as being complete and of the same substance as the other two persons of the Trinity: God the Father and God the Son.

God's big, right? He's huge. Unimaginably gigantatoid. And so we naturally have that sense of God being *out there* somewhere, residing in the heavens, somewhat detachedly overseeing and directing everything that happens everywhere in the universe. We have an intuitive image of God as the Impenetrable, the Inscrutable, the Unknowable.

And that makes sense: We are, after all, talking about the Forever Beyond here, about the Alpha and Omega, the Maker of all that is, has been, and ever will be. No surprise, then, that we have this very profound sense of eternal otherness about God.

And in a very real sense, that *is* who God is. God the Father *is* God above.

But through Jesus Christ, we are given a vastly different way to appreciate and know God. Here is God as also fully human, God as anything but detached from our fears and trials. Here is God loving us so much that he incarnated himself as one of us and then willfully allowed himself to be brutally killed so that we might *begin* to grasp the depth of his commitment to our present and eternal well-being. Even if we can't fully understand the whole of Jesus, we know that as the God-man he has personified human, earthly action, persuasion, conviction, love, anger, anguish . . . that in sending Jesus, God has revealed himself as someone with whom we can definitely relate and even identify. More important, Jesus proves that God is someone who can forever identify with us.

This is a God whom we know knows every last bit of trouble we will ever suffer.

First we have God the Father above us—and then we have God the Son down here on earth, abiding where we live and breathe and die. *God with us.*

But ultimately, physically, Jesus left us, didn't he? After his stunning resurrection, the Son returned to heaven, where, as the

Bible tells us, he resumed his place next to the Father. And then here we are, left without the God in flesh that we once had walking among us.

That breaks our hearts. And over time it's also bound to make it harder for us to properly remember and honor God. We humans are, after all, inclined to be more impressed and persuaded by what's before us than by what seems to be eons behind us.

God, of course, knows this about us. He knows we can't live on memories and ancient stories alone. He knows that in order to keep us inspired and engaged we need something dynamic, immediate, real, vibrant, deeply individualized, and profoundly personal.

And so out of his infinite love for us, he arranged to leave behind in the heart of every one of his believers *the entirety of himself*—that miraculous, clear, unmistakably holy presence inside each of us that we call *the Holy Spirit*.

The Holy Spirit is God within. He's all of God, as close to any believer as his or her next heartbeat.

From John 14 (this is Jesus speaking):

I will ask the Father, and he will give you another
Counselor to be with you forever—the Spirit of truth. The
world cannot accept him, because it neither sees him nor
knows him. But you know him, for he lives with you and
will be in you. I will not leave you as orphans; I will come
to you. . . . But the Counselor, the Holy Spirit, whom
the Father will send in my name, will teach you all things
and will remind you of everything I have said to you. (vv.
16–18, 26)

Mysterious, isn't it? But wonderful. Especially when you begin to call upon the power of the Holy Spirit to assist you in whatever you do.

And now for something a little more complicated: or perhaps not so complicated, if you happen to be someone who is all at once a husband, father, and brother—or a wife, mother, and sister.

How does it make sense that God is at once Father, Son, *and* Holy Spirit?

In the way we usually mean it when we talk about something making sense, the reality of the divine Trinity doesn't make sense at all (to the finite mind). Even the word *trinity* is a graceful melding of fundamentally incompatible concepts: *tri*, meaning three, and *unity*, meaning one. See? *Threeone!* Seems irrational!

The full nature of God is not supposed to be rationally comprehensible to us; that it *isn't* is part and parcel of the majestic mysticism of Christianity. The things in our lives that make sense to us are those wholly contained in our physical, mechanical world. Pencil sharpeners make sense. Leveling off the foundation of a house before you build it makes sense. Flossing your teeth every night makes sense. God, though, is hardly about that kind of logical accessibility; God is not subject to the kinds of objective, verifiable evaluations most everything else in our world is. God *does* make sense; all logic and reason is based upon and born out of his very nature. But God is no more contained or defined by the human notion of "sense" than the Pacific Ocean is contained in or defined by a child's bucket full of seawater.

Think about how much completely vital stuff in your life *doesn't* make "sense." Like sleep, for instance. People have been sleeping since forever, and to this day scientists have just about zero idea what sleeping actually is. Sleep is simply not clear: What it does, why it does it, what it's for. First you're conscious, awake, fully functional, going about your life—and then, as if you've suddenly been unplugged, you lie down and . . . lose consciousness. Except you don't even completely do that. You dream—whatever *that* is.

And what about your heart? Not your physical heart (which, by the way, barely makes sense: Where does the electrical impulse that times it so perfectly come from?) but your other heart, your spiritual heart. Talk about not exactly being logic-based. Your heart wouldn't know logic from Houdini's hairpiece. The human heart isn't about logic. It's about emotion, sensitivity, intuition, spirituality. It's about love. And as everyone who's ever loved anyone else knows, love has no more to do with logic than fish have to do with building pyramids.

Which isn't to say there's no logic in love. There is. For instance, it wouldn't be logical for a suitor to attempt to prove his affections to his beloved by shaving off and eating half the hair on his head. That's just not likely to impress her in the right way. But if the suitor's beloved *asked* him to do that, Mr. Love-Besotted would have a razor in his hand before you could say, "Pass the salsa."

Because that's what love is: vast beyond our reckoning, massively powerful, something that with all of our heart we *must* respond to and even obey.

And as for the essence of this, do you know what Christians believe about God? We believe that God is love. (For the record, in 1 John 4:8, we read this Major Summary: "God is love." Doesn't leave room for a lot of interpretation, does it?)

So there you have it. Despite what you might sometimes think, you would in fact hate much about your life if through the exercise of logic and reason you could understand everything about love. It's the mystery of love that makes it so enrapturing, so intoxicating, so larger-than-life.

Additionally, just as that's true, it's also true that you would definitely not want a God whom you could fully understand through logic and reason. That wouldn't be an awesome, wondrous, formidable God. That would be something more akin to a really complicated math problem.

And as complicated as mathematics can get, it still can't go anywhere near one equaling three.

Another very important creed (besides the Nicene Creed and the others we mentioned earlier in this chapter) is the fifth-century Athanasian Creed. One of this confession's primary purposes was to articulate the profoundly mysterious truth of the triune nature of God. In part, it says: "The Father is God, the Son is God, and the Holy Spirit is God—and yet there are not three Gods, but one God."

And there you have it. Extremely simple; unimaginably complex.

Which instantly brings us back into the middle of God's territory.

Which is to say, back into the middle of life.

Life is so extremely simple.

Life is so unimaginably complex.

God is so extremely simple.

God is so unimaginably complex.

In truth, that the one Godhead should contain the three persons of Father, Son, and Holy Spirit actually makes beautiful, wonderful sense.

After being baptized, Jesus came up immediately from the water; and behold, the heavens were opened, and he saw the Spirit of God descending as a dove and lighting on Him, and behold, a voice out of the heavens said, "This is My beloved Son, in whom I am well-pleased." (Matthew 3:16–17, NASB)

May the grace of the Lord Jesus Christ, and the love of God, and the fellowship of the Holy Spirit be with you all. (2 Corinthians 13:14)

Oh, the depth of the riches of the wisdom and knowledge of God! How unsearchable his judgments, and his paths beyond tracing out! (Romans 11:33)

Yeah, okay—it's hard to grasp. And speaking of hard to grasp, here's another one: How could this all-powerful Creator of all things from nothing be more than all-powerful? Specifically, how could this God, the source of lightning bolts and asteroid collisions, the very source of strength and might, also be a provider of this amazing—and amazingly personal—thing called *grace*?

What does "saved by grace" mean?

Those are the classic three words Protestant Christians use to encapsulate the truth that there are no actions any person can undertake to earn their way into heaven or God's grace. That we are saved not by works but by grace alone—the grace that comes through an unshakable faith in Jesus Christ—is central to the doctrine with which the German theologian Martin Luther profoundly challenged the Catholic Church and which ultimately resulted in the Protestant Reformation.

Read the following carefully. It is the Great Reformer's interpretation of the apostle Paul's words, and it's something all Protestants believe:

"All have sinned and are justified freely, without their own works and merits, by His grace, through the redemption that is in Christ Jesus, in His blood" (Romans 3:23–25). This is necessary to believe. This cannot be otherwise acquired or grasped by any work, law, or merit. Therefore, it is clear and certain that this faith alone justifies us.

It's easy for us to fall into thinking we can earn our way into God's graces—that if we do enough good things, if we behave in righteous ways, if we sacrifice for others, if we give so much money to our church, and so on—then God will smile down upon us, fill us with his Spirit, and save a place for us in heaven.

What makes it so easy for us to think about our relationship to God in such simple, cause-and-effect terms is that down here in our earthly life, reward generally *is* tied to our Actual Performance. If as a student or employee we work extra hard, we get *rewarded* for doing so: We get the "A," we get the accolades, we get the promotion. In our everyday life, "good works" *work:* they get tangible, measurable results.

But God's grace isn't like that. We're not going to impress him by anything we do, no matter how selflessly or nobly we do it. It's not like *we're* ever going to do anything so great that it will cause God to forget the same truths about us that each of us secretly knows about ourselves: that we're forever being selfish, and greedy, and lazy, and opportunistic, and mean-spirited, and . . . well, *sinful.* (See chapter 3, "Everyone: Sin, the Human Constant.") We know it about ourselves; God knows it about us; there's no use pretending either one of us is capable of forgetting it.

A Christian does good works because loving God inspires him (or her) to do good works, not because he hopes it will inspire God to love him. That's just not how it happens. Because how would our earning our way into his goodwill come about? What are *we* going to bring to God? How is *anything* we could ever do going to enhance or benefit the reality of God, in whom *everything* already exists?

God wants one thing from us, and only one thing. He wants us to believe in him. He wants us to believe that out of love, through his fully and finally sufficient sacrifice, he paid the eternal price for the sins of each and every one of us. Believing *that* is what gets us saved; *that* is what triggers to life the life of Christ within us.

In short: If you want God to believe in you, believe in him.

All that said, though, let us never forget or in any way minimize the truth that once one is saved, one is naturally and irresistibly compelled to serve his fellow man—to, in other words, do good works. A man who claims he is saved but who never works for the betterment of others is deluding himself; the Holy Spirit is not in him. In his Great Commandment, Christ directs us to love our neighbor as we love ourselves, and so we must take the time to actually, physically, in real time, do nothing less than that very thing. (For more on this, see the Question, "What is the Great Commandment—and what makes it so great?" on page 69.)

With faith comes grace. With grace comes love. With love comes action.

But always—*necessarily*—faith first.

> We maintain that a man is justified by faith apart from observing the Law. (Romans 3:28)

but also . . .

> As the body without the spirit is dead, so faith without deeds is dead. (James 2:26)

And the Bible's ultimate grace/works Combo Quote:

> It is by grace you have been saved, through faith—and this not from yourselves, it is the gift of God—not by works, so that no one can boast. For we are God's workmanship, created in Christ Jesus to do good works, which God prepared in advance for us to do. (Ephesians 2:8–10)

In our lifetime a great guy named Chuck Colson, who came to understand and receive God's unmerited favor, wrote a book entitled *Born Again*. It's his story about coming out of serving time for a Watergate crime to serving the God of the universe. That book, and its title, introduced those two words to a lot of people. But many who heard them never found out what they really mean.

To what do the words *born again* actually refer?

This term is used to describe a person who has received the ineffably wonderful experience of being saved by Christ. When you realize that he atoned for all your sins on the cross—that in the indescribable, beneficent, sacrificial love of Jesus, you are finally and irrevocably set free and forgiven of your sins—you feel positively and radiantly *reborn*.

Christ gives his believers an entirely, radically new lease on life.

When you become a Christian, your old, sinful, selfish, unrepentant way of life dies.

And there you are, new in Christ.

You're *born again*!

Jesus declared, "I tell you the truth, no one can see the kingdom of God unless he is born again" (John 3:3).

We have said that God is love; that he saves, offers grace, and blasts our world into two parts: BBC (Before Being Christian) and ABC (After Becoming Christian). Even if you know this, though, you may still wonder just how personal God can become to you.

How do I know that God loves me personally?

It *is* hard to believe that God—who is, after all, so vast we can't even begin to imagine how vast—could be as intimately and personally invested in us as . . . well, as individuals. How can such a thing be true?

How can you really be sure that a person loves you? That they love not the idea of you, or the impression of you that you've made upon them, or the you that they're one day hoping you'll become—but actually, *you?*

First, that person has to know you. And the better that person knows you, the more secure you can be in the quality of that person's love for you. If someone really *knows* you, warts and all, and they *still* love you, then you can be sure that person isn't a fair-weather friend or lover, someone who might leave once they find out you don't measure up to some kind of ideal they have for you.

Bottom line: The first criterion for being sure someone really loves you is knowing that they really *know* you.

Well, it's a cinch that God *really* knows you. We are, after all, talking about *God* here. It's entirely safe to state (in an understatement!) that God knows you at least as well as you know yourself. If you think you can hide anything about yourself from the omnipotent, omniscient God Almighty, then . . . good luck with that.

The other thing that has to happen before you can be entirely confident of a person's love for you is that they must do something to prove their love. Talk is cheap. If someone's going to talk the I-love-you talk, then they've got to walk the I-love-you walk. Otherwise, all you have to go on is words.

So let's see. What has God ever done for you personally?

For starters, *Jesus was sacrificially slaughtered as a means of forever paying off the debt of any sins you personally would ever commit.*

Which pretty much wraps that up, don't you think?

But wait! There's more!

God also left behind, in the heart of each and every one of his believers, the entirety of himself in the form of his Spirit. Most people won't leave *Tupperware* behind with people they're not seriously attached to. And here God has arranged to leave *everything he is* behind with you personally, in exchange for your doing nothing more taxing than asking him for it.

And why did God do these things for, specifically and exactly, *you,* whom he knows better than you know yourself?

He allowed himself to be sacrificed and left you his Holy Spirit so that during your time here on earth you could be a satisfied, righteous, spiritually fulfilled person—and so that after you left this earth, you could enjoy the rest of eternity, basking in the wondrous glory that is his unending splendor and love.

And *that,* friend, is how you can be sure God loves you personally.

Christ loved us and gave himself up for us. (Ephesians 5:2)

Even the Son of Man did not come to be served, but to serve, and to give his life as a ransom for many. (Mark 10:45)

God so loved the world, that He gave His only begotten Son, that whoever believes in Him shall not perish, but have eternal life. (John 3:16, NASB)

Are not five sparrows sold for two pennies? Yet not one of them is forgotten by God. Indeed, the very hairs of your head are all numbered. Don't be afraid; you are worth more than many sparrows. (Luke 12:6–7)

When you stop and think about it, you've probably had at least one experience that was just too astonishing to be coincidence, that you knew could only be God reaching into your world to touch your life directly. But if God is personally involved with you, then of course this raises the question of whether or not he has something specific that he wants you to do.

Does God have a plan for me?

He certainly does. God's plan is for you to accept the fact that he loves you, has always loved you, and will always love you. God's plan for you is to trust in the truth of who he is, and in what he has done for you. It's for you to open yourself up to the wondrous powers of the Holy Spirit within you. God's Big Plan is for everyone who believes in him to be gathered around him after they've departed from this vale of tears, and to spend eternity in the utter delight and fulfillment of his incomparable presence.

In a nutshell, God's plan for you is to love him, and to then use that love to serve him and others.

> Praise be to the God and Father of our Lord Jesus Christ,
> who has blessed us in the heavenly realms with every
> spiritual blessing in Christ. For he chose us in him before
> the creation of the world to be holy and blameless in his
> sight. (Ephesians 1:3–4)

In addition to serving God and loving others, there's something else in God's plan. It's a huge part of why he created us, and why he sticks with us even when we mess up. It's called relationship.

How do I deepen my relationship with God?

Simple: You ask *him* that question. In a very real sense, God is waiting for each and every one of us to ask him how we can deepen and enrich our relationship with him.

God has a lot of answers—which figures, considering he has *all* the answers—but for that particular question, he *really* has an answer. And if you sincerely ask him this question, what you are certain to "hear" him communicate to you in one way or another is that you would do well to begin incorporating into your daily life the following four practices:

(1) Listening to God
(2) Reflecting upon God
(3) Being humble before God
(4) Trusting in God

God has a lot of things to say to all of us, but he puts doing those four things into the heart and mind of *anyone* seeking to know him better.

We'll go over them quickly. But before we do, know this: in order to effectively do one or all of these four things, you don't have to be an expert at worship, or anything like that. You don't have to be any holier than you are right now in order to get Maximum Results from undertaking these four basic, foundational steps. Just start doing them—and trust that God will take care of the rest. (Which is doing step four!)

Listening to God

Again, this doesn't mean you have to climb to the top of a mountain and lose yourself in prayer, or kneel in a church for countless hours. It just means that every once in a while—while you're cooking, driving, standing in line at the bank, walking your dog, and so on—simply try opening yourself up to listening to the Holy Spirit within you. God is never *not* talking to you. So give a listen. Trust that you *will* be interested in everything God has to say to you. The more you listen, the more you'll want to listen to what is, after all, a voice that's as close to you as any can possibly be.

> Come near to God and he will come near to you. (James 4:8)

> My sheep listen to my voice; I know them, and they follow me. (John 10:27)

Reflecting Upon God

This is just about the easiest thing in the world to do. God is everywhere manifested: in all of nature, in people of all ages, in all of life. He exists in every moment of your perceived experience. Look into your own soul: There is the holy presence of God! Reflect upon him. Use the fact of God's divine, immediate reality to lift you into the kind of grand contemplation that is one of the sweetest glimpses of the next life afforded any of us in this one.

> In the beginning was the Word, and the Word was with God, and the Word was God. He was with God in the beginning.
> Through him all things were made; without him nothing was made that has been made. In him was life, and that life was the light of men. The light shines in the darkness, but the darkness has not understood it. (John 1:1–5)

Being Humble Before God

Stop to think and feel about who and what you are—about who and what any human being is—in comparison to who and what God is. Sit with that understanding for a while. Appreciate it. Let it grow within you. Let it overwhelm you. Let it drop you to your knees.

> Blessed are the poor in spirit,
>   for theirs is the kingdom of heaven.
> Blessed are those who mourn,
>   for they will be comforted.
> Blessed are the meek,
>   for they will inherit the earth. (Matthew 5:3–5)

Everyone who exalts himself will be humbled, and he who humbles himself will be exalted. (Luke 14:11)

Trusting in God

In those three simple words lie the key to the best, richest, most rewarding life possible. It's hard to elaborate on so perfect a phrase. Trust in God. Do it. Every once in a while—especially if it's been a while—stop whatever you're doing, and hold in your mind and heart the fact that the entirety of everything you ever worry about is in the hands of God, and that everything he does involving you and your world he does so that ultimately you will know the peace of his abiding presence. It has never been any different, and it never will be any different: God loves you, and you can trust him. Stop, take time to relax in that amazing truth, and rejoice in it.

> During the fourth watch of the night Jesus went out to
> them, walking on the lake. When the disciples saw him
> walking on the lake, they were terrified. "It's a ghost,"

they said, and cried out in fear.

But Jesus immediately said to them: "Take courage! It is I. Don't be afraid."

"Lord, if it's you," Peter replied, "tell me to come to you on the water."

"Come," he said.

Then Peter got down out of the boat, walked on the water and came toward Jesus. But when he saw the wind, he was afraid and, beginning to sink, cried out, "Lord, save me!"

Immediately Jesus reached out his hand and caught him. "You of little faith," he said, "why did you doubt?" (Matthew 14:25–31).

As your relationship with God grows through the practice of these four simple endeavors, you'll find yourself increasingly willing to say five life-changing words.

What's the best thing to constantly tell myself in order to always remember my true and proper relationship to God?

These five words: *"Let go, and let God."* It makes a great bumper sticker, and an even greater motto to live by. We Christians have one overarching challenge: to as consistently as possible get ourselves out of the way of what the Holy Spirit is trying to do through and with us. That's not particularly easy or natural for us to do; we are, in fact, almost wholly inclined to *not* let go, and *not* let God. And the degree to which we all cling tenaciously to the idea that we can handle everything that needs handling is understandable: We are, after all, capable, smart, worldly wise beings, whose lives are largely defined by issues and situations we can handle.

So we become the ultimate Do-It-Yourselfers.

We don't want to let go. We *like* imagining that we're in control. We're pretty sure there's nothing we can't overcome.

And then, feeling that way, we forget—or at least keep pushed to the back of our mind—God.

And then, slowly but surely, we discover that not only can we *not* handle everything life tosses our way, but that we are particularly unprepared to handle all the stuff that actually matters most to us. Our relationships sour. Our work goes awry. Our sense of who we are gets skewed. We bumble our responsibilities *and* our privileges.

We find, in short, that we're (still) selfish, greedy, ego-crazed, status-starved, narrow-minded, shameless opportunists. Or something along those lines, anyway.

We find that we're not at all the person we'd been so sure we were.

And then—if we're fortunate; if we're Christian—we come to the place where we ask God to do a personal intervention: to come between the person he made us to be and the person we have made ourselves.

We fall to our knees.

We let go, and let God.

Volunteer to live those words every day, or one day be forced to. It really is that simple.

I have been crucified with Christ and I no longer live, but Christ lives in me. (Galatians 2:20)

Letting go and letting God is never easy. Ask him to help you let go and to let him do for you what you cannot do for yourself. You can never go wrong with that kind of prayer. And remember, letting go and letting God doesn't mean turning into someone who's passive, emotionally disconnected, or in any way fatalistic. It doesn't mean giving up your will; it means *joining* your will to

God's. And that's as active, connected, vital, and life-affirming as anything can possibly be.

What is prayer?

The short answer is that it's deliberately, attentively, and openly turning your mind to God.

The longer answer is that there are in essence two kinds of prayers: meditative and intentional. Meditative prayer is when one brings oneself to God with no explicit purpose beyond simply being with him—communing with him, *listening* to him. Meditative prayer is not about results; it's purely about the experience of being with God.

Intentional prayer is the sort of interaction with God that most people mean when they use the word *prayer*. This is where one brings oneself before God with an end in mind; it's what we do when we appeal to God for his help with a problem, or with a concern that we know we alone are incapable of satisfactorily resolving.

Generally, an intentional prayer will boil down to one of four core types: supplication ("Lord, I'm humbly asking you for this thing"); contrition ("Lord, I so deeply regret what I've done"); intercession ("Lord, I'm asking for you to get directly involved, and turn this bad situation into something good"); and finally, pure, good ol' fashioned gratitude ("Thanks, Lord, for looking out for me").

Books can be (and, goodness knows, have been) written about the reasons it's spiritually, psychologically, and even materially beneficial to pray. (Prayer is beneficial materially because, for instance, more prayer = less stress = a clearer mind = more productivity.) The main thing about prayer is it's an act that puts you in your proper, natural relationship with God. In the very best possible way, praying puts a person in their place—that is, in the best place anyone *can* be, which is before God with an attitude of humility, hopefulness, appreciation, and love.

In life, proper context is everything: You can't know who you are or what you're doing without understanding the context in which you're existing and acting. The great thing about praying—whether it's meditative or intentional—is that it centers you at the humming, vibrant balance point between yourself and the created universe, and the infinite, infinitely powerful, infinitely compassionate being who created it.

> If you remain in me and my words remain in you, ask whatever you wish, and it will be given you. (John 15:7)

> This is the confidence we have in approaching God: that if we ask anything according to his will, he hears us. And if we know that he hears us—whatever we ask—we know that we have what we asked of him. (1 John 5:14–15)

> Do not be anxious about anything, but in everything, by prayer and petition, with thanksgiving, present your requests to God. (Philippians 4:6)

Once you have a good sense of what prayer is, you'll naturally want to learn how to do it better and experience it more fully.

How do I pray?

Well, imagine for a moment that you're God. (But *only* for a moment: God only knows how much trouble and pain has come from people who've spent a little too much time imagining they're God!) If you were the creator of the universe, how do you think you'd want people to pray to you?

Seriously, right? You'd want them to *mean* it.

42

The main thing about praying is that we approach God with earnest sincerity and heartfelt faith.

As far as how to pray physically—well, again, imagine that you're God. Would you think much of someone popping out two-second petitions to you between phone calls while they're driving and punching buttons on their XM radio? If that was someone's main way of relating to you, would that honor you and please you? Or would you prefer the prayer of someone who before approaching you, settled down, took a moment to be alone, closed their eyes, maybe got down on their knees and bowed their head—someone who behaved the way people naturally do when they're involved in something sacred, awesome, and vital to their interests. Much better, right?

Get down on your knees to pray, and you *will* have God's attention. But of course that classic pose is hardly indispensable to the act of praying. God will be just as pleased if you simply sit quietly and comfortably, take a few deep breaths, calm your spirit, open yourself up to the love and faith you have in him, and then present yourself and your cares before him. (Consider designating part of your home—a quiet room or a quiet corner—as the place where you regularly pray. Keep your Bible there and perhaps a notebook to jot down ideas or thoughts as they surface during your prayer time. You'll find that having a specific place for prayer serves as its own kind of comfort and even inspiration.)

Finally, you'll often hear Christians end their prayers with a variation of the phrase, "We ask this in the name of our Lord, Jesus Christ." The impetus behind this comes straight out of the Bible; in John 16:23, Jesus says, "I tell you the truth, my Father will give you whatever you ask in my name." And the reason it makes such providential sense to ask for our prayers to be answered in the name of Jesus is because it was *Jesus* who sacrificed himself for our eternal betterment, *Jesus* who willingly became the intermediary redeemer for all humankind.

As corporeal beings we naturally go through the tangible, physical reality of Jesus the Son to reach the intangible, spiritual entity of God the Father. (And that's also why a prayer concluding with "in the name of our Lord, Jesus Christ" usually begins with the word *Father*—because in this way the supplication moves from beseeching the Father to invoking the Son. And "Our Lord" is a wonderful way to reference the Spirit—which means that in a typical prayer, all three members of the Trinity are called upon. [For more on the Trinity, refer again to the Question, "How does it make sense that God is at once Father, Son, *and* Holy Spirit?" on page 26.])

> If you believe, you will receive whatever you ask for in prayer. (Matthew 21:22)

> Praise be to the Lord, the God of Israel, because he has come and has redeemed his people. (Luke 1:68)

Don't forget: The more you practice prayer as a habit that you conduct in different forms throughout the day, the more effective you'll be at integrating prayer into your life. But some people get hung up on needing to be perfect before they begin to pray.

Do I have to be "pure" before I can come before God?

This is certainly an understandable and even very touching question, but the bottom line is that if everyone waited until they were pure of spirit and/or body before coming to God in prayer, God would have so much free time on his hands (metaphorically speaking) that he'd probably create a whole new race of beings who *are* pure, just so he'd have someone to talk to. But until he does that, God is stuck with us, and the absolute *purest* among us (whoever that might be) is still, at their core, so selfish, fallen, and full of sin that their only hope is the same as ours: to humbly come before God and beseech him for his mercy.

Certainly no man is so pure of heart and spirit that he *deserves* to come before God. We turn to God for our salvation not because we are worthy of that salvation but because God has freely offered it to us despite our sinful nature. (For more on sin, see the Questions, "What is sin?" and "What is 'original sin'?" on pages 109 and 111.)

The point is: In this lifetime, none of us can ever be *pure*. The word actually has no meaning relative to the state of the human soul or consciousness. Water can be pure. Heroin can be pure (pure evil, that is). Gold can be pure. All any of *us* can be is an impenetrable, undecipherable, ever-fluctuating mass of infinite contradictions. And *that's* on a good day.

Besides, God isn't interested in anyone who thinks they're "pure" (given how unlikely it is that such a person would have any interest in him in the first place: why would they?). God wants broken, lost, desperate, self-esteem-lacking, deeply *tweaked* people to come before him, to believe in him, to present themselves to him, to finally ask him for the miraculous grace of his healing salvation. Even people who barely know anything at all about the Bible know that Jesus, the Gentle Healer, preferred the company of prostitutes, winos, and blood-sucking, vulture-like tax collectors over the company of those who were considered "the purest of people": the righteously pious, the religiously scrupulous, the "wise" and educated leaders.

The self-professed pure people are the *only* ones in the Bible toward whom Jesus ever showed out-and-out fury. Everyone else— all the average, *broken* people—he embraced. In fact, the less obviously lovable someone seemed to be, the more Jesus seemed to love them.

Never, ever fear that you're too "impure" to, whenever you're ready, fall on your knees before God. God loves everyone, at any time, exactly as they are. Period.

When the sun was setting, the people brought to Jesus all who had various kinds of sickness, and laying his hands on each one, he healed them. (Luke 4:40)

As Jesus was on his way, the crowds almost crushed him. And a woman was there who had been subject to bleeding for twelve years, but no one could heal her. She came up behind him and touched the edge of his cloak, and immediately her bleeding stopped.

"Who touched me?" Jesus asked.

When they all denied it, Peter said, "Master, the people are crowding and pressing against you."

But Jesus said, "Someone touched me; I know that power has gone out from me."

Then the woman, seeing that she could not go unnoticed, came trembling and fell at his feet. In the presence of all the people, she told why she had touched him and how she had been instantly healed.

Then he said to her, "Daughter, your faith has healed you. Go in peace" (Luke 8:42–48).

Jesus went out and saw a tax collector by the name of Levi sitting at his tax booth. "Follow me," Jesus said to him, and Levi got up, left everything and followed him.

Then Levi held a great banquet for Jesus at his house, and a large crowd of tax collectors and others were eating with them. But the Pharisees and the teachers of the law who belonged to their sect complained to his disciples, "Why do you eat and drink with tax collectors and 'sinners'?"

Jesus answered them, "It is not the healthy who need a doctor, but the sick" (Luke 5:27–31).

Once you realize that in order to pray you don't have to pass a purity requirement, you might want to know whether or not you're obligated to pray in public or at any other time.

Should I "say grace" before every meal?

Unless you're comfortable being the sort of person who doesn't thank another person when they do something nice (not to mention life-affirming) for you, then yes, you should say grace—which is to say, give thanks—to God before each meal.

Because you don't want to be the sort of person who doesn't show gratitude when it's deserved, do you? The sort of person who fails to show appreciation for something wonderful? The sort of person who's so sure they deserve whatever great gifts come their way that it doesn't even occur to them to be grateful for those gifts?

Of course you don't want to be that sort of person. No one does.

So you're stuck. Your intrinsic, basic sense of goodness and right demands that every time you eat or drink anything—but especially if you're about to enjoy anything as bountiful as a sit-down meal—you stop for a moment, and give thanks where thanks are definitely due.

A more pragmatic reason to become comfortable with regularly giving thanks before meals is that saying grace is what Christians do. And this means that sooner or later, Christians with whom you're eating are going to show their love and respect for you by suggesting that you take the lead and say the prayer.

It's such a sweet and humbling moment when someone with whom you're about to break bread says, "Will you say grace for us?"

That moment can, however, feel just a tad less than lovely if you know you're going to have to wing that prayer, and you're not really comfortable doing so. Some people—and those people tend to be older, wiser, more experienced Christians—regularly "wing" their before-meal prayers with eloquence and poignancy. There are lots of veteran believers out there who really know how to extemporaneously nail a prayer.

To be safe, though, especially if you're at the beginning of your life as a Christian, we hereby Officially Urge you to memorize one of the following two classic, short, always appropriate Before-Meal Prayers.

The first is so short a parrot could memorize it:

Bless us, O Lord,
and these thy gifts
which we are about to receive from thy bounty,
through Christ our Lord, Amen.

You can't go wrong saying that prayer before a meal, or the traditional, heart-swelling winner below. This is John's personal Before-Meal Prayer of choice; it always feels to him especially touching and trenchant when dining out:

Dear Lord, thank you for this food.
Bless the hands that prepared it.
Bless it to our use and us to your service,
and make us ever mindful of the needs of others.
Through Christ our Lord we pray. Amen.

Pure gold—every time.

Having said all that, don't feel bad about simply telling God, "Hey, thanks for this food and everything else you give to me." He'll hear that one too. God hears all our prayers . . . it's just that sometimes he doesn't answer them the way we were hoping for.

What's it mean when my prayers go unanswered?

At the very least it means you've come up against the mystery of God. And as frustrating and even painful as it can be to experience firsthand, the fact that God is inscrutable must, in the final analysis, be understood as a primary and necessary feature of the divine.

We must always remember that we don't know God exhaustively. We can't. If we could fully know God, then we'd have on our hands a God whom we probably wouldn't *care* to know all that well. Because then we'd have a God who, before too long, would be bound to be something very near to boring.

No one is awed by anything they can totally understand and predict.

If you want an awesome God (and you do! you do!), then you're going to have to be okay with sometimes not being privy to the how's and why's of everything he does.

What you want, then, see, is a God who's both awesome *and loving*. If you're going to have a God who's not so utterly transparent that you can tell everything he's going to do—that is, a God for whom infinite mystery is a primary characteristic— then you *definitely* want a God upon whom you can depend to do whatever he does out of love for you.

And welcome, once again, to Christianity.

God does love you, always. And you can trust him, always.

That said, however, sometimes your prayers are not in any apparent way going to be answered. And a lot of those times you won't have any idea why God chose not to fulfill your stated desires in such a way that you could attribute that satisfaction to his direct intervention.

After you leave this earth, you'll know exactly why God handled each of your prayers exactly as he did. Then everything will be revealed to you. Until then, however, all you can do when a prayer hasn't been answered is contemplate why God might have chosen to respond to your request with silence.

First off, consider the possibility that when you were praying the prayer in question, your heart wasn't truly into it. That happens. With our desires we're sometimes like a little kid who *seems* as if he or she really, really wants something—who, in fact, at the time is *positive* that they really, really want that thing. But you know how that is. Sometimes when kids are super intense about getting something they want, they squeeze their eyes shut real tight, get hyper-focused, and basically act like if they don't get what they're begging for, the entire universe will get sucked into the giant black hole caused by their not having it.

Sometimes when that happens, you know the kid's desires are temporary—that they have more to do with drama (or peer pressure, or boredom, or over-stimulation) than with any sort of genuine need.

And of course knowing that their passion is essentially transitory renders you less inclined than you might be otherwise to grant that child their wish.

So maybe when you prayed for that thing you never got, or that event that never happened, God knew you didn't *really* want it all that much anyway.

But let's say you prayed earnestly for something that wasn't frivolous, and your prayer still went unanswered. This disappointment is a little more serious.

What must be said, though, is that this disappointment is also founded upon a supposition that bears some examining. The supposition is that *you* know what desires God should and shouldn't fulfill. That is one . . . beefy premise. Again (we know, borderline insultingly) we look to the child as a metaphor. Sometimes what kids want at a given time isn't what's actually going to work best for them in the long run: a pocketful of candy. A Mohawk haircut. A forehead tattoo. Their own Hummer. You know the sorts of things we mean.

It certainly seems like a secure bet that sometimes God doesn't answer our prayers because he's aware that his, ours, and the whole *world's* best interests will not be served if he does.

Safe to say that when God decides what's best, he's got a broader perspective for making that decision than anything we can bring to the table.

All of which brings us to the very good reason that when mature Christians do pray for something, they tend not to say, "God, please do [such and such]," but rather, "God, *if it is your will,* please do [such and such]." This is the all-important caveat. Always leave to him the final determination of whether or not what you're asking for is, in fact, the thing most ultimately beneficial.

Besides being the Obvious Best Judge of what is and isn't best for us and the world at large, God, in his unending benevolence, also tends to grant us a great deal more than we would have ever dared request. Being in a relationship with God means that if you earnestly pray for one hundred dollars he's just as likely to bring you a thousand!

But bringing you that thousand dollars might take a little more *time.* And God will use that time. He knows the time he takes to answer your prayer is time that you have available to give him. God knows your life. And part of that is knowing when it's best for you to wait on whatever he has in mind for you.

So be slow to reach the pessimistic conclusion that God has failed to "answer" one of your prayers. Let things unfold awhile. See what happens. Given time, you'll very often find that God *has* answered your prayers, but in ways so far beyond what you actually prayed that you hadn't even noticed how richly and abundantly your prayer has been answered.

For example, maybe you'll pray and pray to find your lost bus pass, and that pass will remain lost—but then, a month later, you'll somehow, through some miracle, get a new car.

Besides (1) not really wanting whatever you prayed for, (2) praying for what wasn't actually the best thing, or (3) your prayer later being answered in ways you couldn't begin to imagine, there's at least one more possible reason for "unanswered" prayer. While we never *deserve* to have our prayers answered, your prayer might go unanswered because you've been living as though you don't deserve an answer.

Think about it: No matter how you cut it, when you pray for something, you *are* asking God for a favor.

And who's most likely to do you a favor you've asked for: a friend, an acquaintance, or an enemy?

If ever you find yourself wondering why God hasn't replied to a prayer, ask yourself whether, to him, you've been more of a friend, an acquaintance, or an enemy.

Have you respected God? Do you regularly turn to him for counsel and advice? Do you live your life in such a way that he has reason to be proud of your association with him? Do you act like one of his ambassadors, or one of his errant children?

Have you been treating Jesus like the friend he has shown himself to be to you?

Maybe by not simply handing over whatever you've asked for, God is disciplining you. That's his prerogative.

Be a better friend to him, and maybe he'll be a better—well, a more *obviously* better—friend to you.

One thing you can be assured of: God *always* hears your prayers. Once you pray that connection has been made.

God hears your prayers; God does with your prayers whatever he knows is best for you and the world at large.

That's God. That's what God *does*.

Trust in him.

I tell you, do not worry about your life, what you will
eat or drink; or about your body, what you will wear. Is
not life more important than food, and the body more
important than clothes? Look at the birds of the air; they
do not sow or reap or store away in barns, and yet your
heavenly Father feeds them. Are you not much more
valuable than they? Who of you by worrying can add a
single hour to his life?

And why do you worry about clothes? See how the
lilies of the field grow. They do not labor or spin. Yet I tell
you that not even Solomon in all his splendor was dressed
like one of these. If that is how God clothes the grass of
the field, which is here today and tomorrow is thrown into
the fire, will he not much more clothe you, O you of little
faith? So do not worry, saying, "What shall we eat?" or
"What shall we drink?" or "What shall we wear?" For the
pagans run after all these things, and your heavenly Father
knows that you need them. But seek first his kingdom and
his righteousness, and all these things will be given to you
as well. (Matthew 6:25–33)

Peace I leave with you; My peace I give to you; not as
the world gives do I give to you. Do not let your heart be
troubled, nor let it be fearful. (John 14:27, NASB)

There's just no other way to experience deep and lasting peace
than by being in constant contact with God through prayer. As
you continue to communicate with him, you will become increasingly aware that he is with you, has always been with you, and
will be with you forever.

How do I discern the presence of God around me at any time?

It's unlikely that anywhere in this book will we be faced with a question that's easier to answer than this one.

Woo-hoo! Gotta love the view from here on Easy Street!

Speaking of key views, the answer to how you can at any time discern God's presence around you is to simply extend your senses to your surroundings, and then pay attention to whatever those senses register.

In other words: You discern the presence of God simply by looking around.

Do it. Give it a shot right now. Stop reading, and look around.

Do you know what you just saw? *God!*

Because we so readily and naturally take for granted the physical world around us, it is sometimes difficult to remember that God isn't *only* in heaven, or in church, or even in our hearts by the Holy Spirit. God is unceasingly striving (insofar as God *strives* to do anything) to in every possible way communicate to us the immediate reality of his presence. He does that inside of us—and he does it outside of us.

When at any given time you stop to simply gaze around you, what do you see? You see patterns: light. Forms. Textures. Layers upon layers of natural and man-made phenomena. You see color. You see things that on an atomic level are zinging around like crazy—and yet there they are, frozen in time and space, solid as can be.

And if at any point in your day you stop to really *listen*, what do you hear? You hear the music of life; the rich, unending, multi-layered hum of existence.

And what do you touch? What do you smell? What do you taste? In every case, you experience sensations and have experiences so profound and complex that science must ultimately throw up its hands before it all, and admit that reason and experimentation cannot grasp what is most essential and elemental about life.

What each and every one of us has all the time, everywhere around us, is flat-out, 100 percent *miracle*. (Which is not to in any way denigrate science. Do any of us really want to think of where we'd be without the human capacity and propensity for applying reason to the physical universe?)

If you want to experience God, stop for a moment—any moment, anywhere, any time—and . . . well . . . experience God!

That's what you're *designed* to do. That's what the world is *designed* to inspire in you.

Yes, we are fallen, and no, we won't experience perfection or perfect harmony until Jesus returns to fully and finally right all wrongs. Still, though, the world—billboards, air pollution, and the harping, jagged detritus of modern life notwithstanding—was created to inspire awe in us. Dust it for prints with your senses, and *everywhere* you will see, hear, smell, taste, and touch the signs of its Maker.

People who are resistant to the idea of believing in God often say how they *would* believe in God, if just once in their life they could see or experience a true, undeniable miracle.

And yet, they are constantly and everywhere surrounded by nothing but miracles.

The real question is never "Where is God?" The real question is where isn't he?

God is nowhere? No. God is now here.

Through him all things were made; without him nothing was made that has been made. (John 1:3)

By him [Jesus] all things were created: things in heaven and on earth, visible and invisible, whether thrones or powers or rulers or authorities; all things were created by him and for him. He is before all things, and in him all things hold together. (Colossians 1:16–17)

While some people say they would believe in God if he made his presence known, it's important to remember that when he did, people killed him. Even when God in the form of Jesus was walking around on earth, you still had to have faith that he existed when things were good or when things were very, very bad. And in this world there is going to be an awful lot of bad.

Why does God allow evil to exist?

This is a tough question; it is, in fact, so tough that for centuries it has comprised its own specific, dedicated field of study. The branch of theological and philosophical inquiry that seeks to reconcile evil with a just and benevolent God is called *theodicy*—i.e., the problem of evil.

Just asking this question makes you a theodicean.

Sure, you knew reading this book would make you smarter. But did you think it would make you a theodicean?

You did not.

Don't lie.

Because lying is evil, and . . . well, what are we telling *you* for? *You're* the theodicean.

Okay. Here's our Official Take on why God allows evil to exist:

God allows evil to exist because he allows *people* to exist. It's people who do evil, not God. (Here we are specifically discussing Human-Generated Evil. We'll deal with so-called "natural evil"—earthquakes and floods and cancer and so on—in the next question, below. [And we'll talk about the spiritual origin of sin under the Question, "What is 'original sin'?" on page 111.])

What people at heart almost always really mean when they ask, "Why does God allow evil to exist?" is "Why doesn't God stop evil from happening?"—which, in practical terms, necessarily boils down to the question, "Why doesn't God stop people from doing evil things?"

God doesn't stop any of us from doing what we want to do because doing so would require his taking back the free will he gave us. Because he loves us (not to mention that he created us in his image), violating our free will is not something that God is going to do. And it's definitely not anything any of us would *want* God to do. Our free will is what makes us human. It's God's ultimate gift to us; it is *the* quality that defines us. Our free will is proof positive that God loves us so much that he endowed us with the ability to completely ignore or deny him if we want to. *That* is love.

God would have to love us a lot less than he does in order to start overthrowing our free will. He'd have to hate us, in fact.

It's an extremely safe bet that if God ever decided to stop people from doing evil, not a person on this planet wouldn't yearn for the days when they were free to choose. Not that any of us would be able to *have* such a thought, since if God determined that we couldn't think about or do anything he didn't like, we would turn into zombified automatons, deadheads utterly devoid of anything we now recognize as thought. Stopping people from being able to do evil would mean stopping them from *thinking* about doing evil, which would mean stopping them from ever having the negative thoughts that necessarily precede evil actions. And that could *only* result in full mind control.

When does a thought become "evil"? If I think a person is wearing clothes that look bad, is that an evil thought? If I think that person shouldn't have left home wearing those clothes, does that thought now qualify as evil? If I wonder how they could possibly look in the mirror and think they look okay, is *that* thought finally evil? You see the problem. The whole range of thoughts between "not evil" and "evil" constitutes a gray scale of such infinite shade gradation that virtually the only way to stop all evil thoughts (which, remember, necessarily precede evil actions) is to stop all thoughts, period.

Do no evil = think no evil = have no thoughts = the absence of life as we know it.

This is why no one *really* wants God to stop people from doing evil. That evil exists doesn't prove that God isn't benevolent. It proves just how benevolent he is.

> Do not be overcome by evil, but overcome evil with good. (Romans 12:21)

> Submit yourselves, then, to God. Resist the devil, and he will flee from you. (James 4:7)

> Jesus said to him, "Away from me, Satan! For it is written: 'Worship the Lord your God, and serve him only.' " Then the devil left him, and angels came and attended him. (Matthew 4:10–11)

> He causes his sun to rise on the evil and the good, and sends rain on the righteous and the unrighteous. (Matthew 5:45)

Yep, as humans we can make choices that are so bad in so many ways that they can only be classified as evil. But there are other kinds of evil existing in the world today too.

Why does God allow "natural" evil— earthquakes and disease and so on—to exist?

Another good question! How do you keep coming up with these?

Seriously—you have a gift.

Use it for good, friend, and never for evil.

Speaking of which!

We've got the kind of people-to-people evil we looked at above, and then we've got what seems to be God-to-people evil: hurricanes, floods, and the like.

So the question at hand boils down to this: How can a loving God allow people to suffer from terrible things that *aren't* caused by other people?

In response, for starters, we want to be absolutely clear that God hates it when people suffer. Jesus *fully* identifies with us; when we suffer, he suffers. He proved that on the cross.

Here's the bottom line on "natural" evil: We have no idea how much of it could be eradicated by us, right here on earth, if we all together would decide that we care about nothing so much as the health and well-being of every single person on this planet.

We don't know what we could do if we dedicated everything we have to a sustained, worldwide, everyone-on-board effort to eradicate sickness and disease, and to anticipate and manage all "natural" disasters.

We don't know what about our environment and health we're really capable of regulating or controlling; we've never found out because we've always been so busy spending so very, very much of our time, energy, and resources fighting one another.

We simply have no right to blame God for what, for all we know, are problems we could eradicate if we only deepened our commitment to loving our neighbors as we love ourselves—if we gave our all for the betterment of others. (For more on the Great Commandment, see the Question, "What is the Great Commandment—and what makes it so great?" on page 69.)

Every day, for instance, some sixteen thousand children die for want of food. And yet we know there's more than enough food on earth to keep each and every one of us full and healthy.

Who *knows* what we could do if we overhauled our priorities? Who knows how quickly we could cure every disease that now plagues and undermines us?

None of us knows because we've never really made that our priority.

No fair reaching up to God when we've yet to reach out to one another.

> Everyone who hears these words of mine and puts them into practice is like a wise man who built his house on the rock. The rain came down, the streams rose, and the winds blew and beat against that house; yet it did not fall, because it had its foundation on the rock. But everyone who hears these words of mine and does not put them into practice is like a foolish man who built his house on sand. The rain came down, the streams rose, and the winds blew and beat against that house, and it fell with a great crash. (Matthew 7:24–27)

> Jesus answered, "If you want to be perfect, go, sell your possessions and give to the poor, and you will have treasure in heaven. Then come, follow me." When the young man heard this, he went away sad, because he had great wealth. (Matthew 19:21–22)

It's interesting that when something bad happens we conclude it must have been God's intention or fault. Often it's our own. Consider this: In 2004, global sales of cosmetics and toiletries were over $250 billion. What if we all just cut back by a mere 10 percent, or 1/10th? That *$25,000,000,000* could put quite a dent in world hunger and disaster relief, don't you think? And *still* leave you smelling good and looking your best.

We know, all the same, that evil is tough and loss is painful and any tragedy is tough to get over, especially if you believe God should have prevented it.

How do I keep believing in God after what seems to be a senseless tragedy?

You close your eyes, you turn to the Holy Spirit within you, and you ask God if he's still there, if he's still real, if he's still watching out for you and everyone else in the world. If the tragedy with which you're dealing involves the death of someone you love, then you ask God if he or she is all right—if they're safe, and with him now. If you are not sure, leave them with God, who knows every heart and does all things well.

When dealing with a tragedy, it is important to know that bad things happen for many reasons. We live in a fallen world; we have freedom of choice; some people do the wrong thing and we can end up being hurt. We often blame God for things he did not cause. Don't listen to those who might say God had a purpose for causing your tragedy. God will bring purpose from it, and no tear will be wasted. He never promised a life free of pain, but when we are going through it his love for us must cause him to weep with us.

What we can't fathom now *will* be clear to us later.

So sometimes we must simply hang on, and wait for that knowledge.

We are hard pressed on every side, but not crushed;
perplexed, but not in despair; persecuted, but not
abandoned; struck down, but not destroyed. We always
carry around in our body the death of Jesus, so that the
life of Jesus may also be revealed in our body. For we who
are alive are always being given over to death for Jesus'
sake, so that his life may be revealed in our mortal body.
(2 Corinthians 4:8–11)

God is greater than our hearts, and he knows everything.
(1 John 3:20)

Tragedy is, well, always a tragedy. And we can get caught up in a world of what was and what might have been and never discover all that God has for us. Whatever the tragedy, we must grieve the loss and pain and embrace the reality of life before us. The Good News is that after the tragedy God is there for us, because he loves us, and he is real.

If God is real, why doesn't he once and for all just *prove* it?

God doesn't "prove" he exists in ways that are empirically or objectively verifiable for the same reason he doesn't stop people from doing evil: doing so would violate the free will he gave us. (Review the Question, "Why does God allow evil to exist?" on page 56.)

Think about it: What anyone asking this question really wants is for God not only to prove to them *personally* that he exists, but to simultaneously prove his existence to a whole bunch of other people. Because if God proves himself only to you, and to no one else, then that's going to leave you with one whopper of a challenge, isn't it? The moment God proves himself to you and you alone, your choices boil down to exactly two: either tell people how God proved to you that he's real, and somehow satisfactorily explain why he did so to only *you* (and then have them thinking you're absolutely badoinkers), or *don't* tell anyone how God proved to you that he's real, and risk having stress-induced heart failure from having to keep such an extraordinary experience locked up inside.

Either way, you lose.

And that is why claiming to want irrefutable, objectively verifiable proof of God's existence *must* entail your also wanting God to prove he exists to everyone else in the world—or at least to half of them, so that you'll be in the majority.

And what God proving the reality of his existence to everyone in the world at once boils down to is his doing something along the lines of suddenly appearing in the sky, and in a booming voice announcing (something like), "Hello, world! Surprise! It's me! Try not to faint!"

And of course he'd have to say whatever he said in every language. Including, come to think of it, baby talk.

Point is: For God to prove the reality of his existence to everyone in the world at the same time would prove quite the logistical challenge.

And do you know what would happen if God *did* finally and irrefutably prove his existence to everyone at once? People everywhere would scream, faint, exclaim, confess, tear their hair, rend their clothes—and then, after about fifteen minutes, everyone would become so terribly bored with their life that they'd slump over and pass out.

The truth is we *don't* want God to prove he's real to us in the same way everything else in our lives that's "real" to us is real to us. Because his doing so would destroy within us that exquisite, vital, existential *wonderment* that keeps us ever moving forward toward resolution, knowledge, clarity, context, wholeness. And without that quality, without that *drive,* would any of us really be human at all?

Just imagine it. Imagine that God really appeared before you, in physical form—that he spoke, and talked, and just . . . hung out at your place awhile.

You'd be awed and amazed.

And then you'd be freakishly listless. Because *there'd be no mystery left in your life.*

Who remains engaged by a novel they already know the ending to?

We *need* God to be mysterious. In order for us to have the richest, most human experience possible *in this life and on this earth*, we need God to remain just beyond our rational comprehension, just outside our grasp.

Our relationship with God needs to be a two-way, interactive, give-and-take, constantly *exchanging* sort of relationship—of essentially the same sort as we have with everyone else in our lives. If God just appeared to all of us at once, the fundamentals of our personal relationship to him would be radically altered— we'd be so thoroughly pushed out of the subjective give-and-take role that's necessary to keep us engaged with God—that ... that we'd no longer be who we are.

We'd be . . . Unplugged. Frozen. Stopped.

We move forward in our lives because we want to *know*.

If we *did* know, we'd stop.

If we had it all, what would we strive for?

It'd be game over.

Purpose accomplished.

Mystery solved.

No particular reason to go on.

How would that be good?

So you don't, actually, want God to "prove" his existence, any more than you'd want to lose your imagination, your initiative, or your curiosity.

Here's another reason it actually doesn't make any sense to desire that God suddenly prove to everyone that he "really" exists: It's not his purpose to work with all people at once, from the outside, in the same way. God develops his relationship with us individually, from the inside: God speaks to *our* heart, to *our* soul, to *our* experience, in the ways *we* most need to hear and understand him. God loves each one of us personally, and he wants to communicate that intimately, carefully, delicately; he wants to communicate about himself to us in the ways and at the times that are best for us.

For now, God has no interest in simultaneously overwhelming everyone.

God is pleased to be "real" where he can be the *most* real—where you can comprehend the most of him—which is inside of you. We're not just physical beings; part of our being made "in God's image" means we are spiritual, as God is first and foremost spiritual. The fullest communion with him must happen spiritually. It must happen inside of us.

The bottom line is that while you might *think* you want God to objectively, tangibly, concretely, *physically* "prove" his existence, you don't actually want that at all.

You don't want that because you're more complex than that. You don't want that because your needs are more real than that.

You don't want that because you're better than that.

Since the creation of the world God's invisible qualities—
his eternal power and divine nature—have been clearly
seen, being understood from what has been made, so that
men are without excuse. (Romans 1:20)

Surely I am with you always, to the very end of the age.
(Matthew 28:20)

All these questions about God's existence and why the world operates the way it does will ultimately be answered when we get to heaven. But until then we can be grateful that God does exist. If he did not exist—and if people did not change their ways and surrender to him—things would surely be a great deal worse than they are. And we would more clearly see all the bad things that never happened because God's goodness, grace, and love held them back. Until we enter that next life, we want to make the absolute most of this one. And we do that best by holding on to God, ourselves, and others.

CHAPTER TWO

God, You, and Others

⋘⊁

Every one of us does pretty well when we're alone. It's in relationship that we tend to mess up the most, that we truly experience conflict and struggle. Grizzly Adams, living in the wilderness, had to fight with bears, but he never had to contend with someone who was a bear to live with.

Relationship is tough, especially considering that we need to always be relating to others in a way that reflects God's love for them. Among other things, this pretty much eliminates holding up signs that state "God Hates _____" (fill in the blank). To those who hoist such signs, I've often wanted to hold up my own that says, "God Hates People Who Hold Up Signs Saying He Hates People." But that would not be, well, very godly. And it sure wouldn't reflect God's attitude toward those who don't think or believe exactly like me.

What should my attitude be toward Christians whose ideas or understanding of Christianity is different from mine?

In a word, respectful.

In two words, respectful and understanding.

In . . . more words: It's not up to you to determine where a person is in their journey toward God. You can believe that you know the truth, and if you do, that truth will motivate you to understand what others believe to be true. Rather than first trying to correct them, you'll hopefully try to connect with them, as Jesus so often did.

That said, we know how just-about-impossible it is *not* to judge the religiosity and/or theology of another. All of us, by instinct, believe with all our heart that the truths about himself that God has placed inside us is *the* truth: the real truth, the big truth, the truer truth, the . . . *better* truth.

Which, of course, can only mean one thing about those who don't share our exact understanding of God and his will.

At best, they're just . . . wrong.

And *religiously* wrong, of course, is never too far from heretical.

And that's a tough word to go anywhere near.

Better not to. Better to simply do your best to draw as near to God as you can and pray for others to do the same.

Do not judge, or you too will be judged. (Matthew 7:1)

The bottom line is that a lot of people we want to judge are actually, literally doing the best they can or the best they know how. Besides, we won't have time to judge everybody who's not as wonderful as we are if we're busy carrying out something great that we're commanded to do.

What is the Great Commandment— and what makes it so great?

As you're surely aware, Jesus taught and said a great many things. Some are easy enough for us to grasp ("If any one of you is without sin, let him be the first to throw a stone at her" [John 8:7]); some are pretty deep ("The Son of Man has no place to lay his head" [Matthew 8:20]); and some are a true challenge ("If anyone comes to me and does not hate his father and mother, his wife and children, his brothers and sisters—yes, even his own life—he cannot be my disciple" [Luke 14:26]).

And then, in Mark 12:28–31, we have this Jesus moment:

> One of the teachers of the law came and heard them [Jesus and some of his critics] debating. Noticing that Jesus had given them a good answer, he asked him, "Of all the commandments, which is the most important?"
>
> "The most important one," answered Jesus, "is this: 'Hear, O Israel, the Lord our God, the Lord is one. Love the Lord your God with all your heart and with all your soul and with all your mind and with all your strength.' The second is this: 'Love your neighbor as yourself.' There is no commandment greater than these."

So. There you have Jesus flat-out telling us what he deems the most important of all his teachings.

Seems like a good thing to pay attention to, doesn't it?

Yes.

If Jesus says that something is the *greatest commandment of all,* then you know you've found ground upon which you can stand the rest of your life, without once having to wonder whether or not you're in the right place.

So the first and most obvious answer to "What makes the Great Commandment so great?" is that Jesus very explicitly told us it isn't just a *good* commandment.

Which, of course, pretty much settles that.

And doesn't it make a lot of sense that if God is love, then the greatest of all the commandments would have a lot to do with exactly that? But a lot of people feel anything but loved because we aren't loving them. So let's get busy doing what we know we need to do, and want to do—and what God wants us to do.

How do I do the Great Commandment?

Like so much of what Jesus taught us, the Great Commandment *seems* really simple—and it is—but it's also so deep, and so rich, that it's like a claim you can keep mining, for pure gold, forever.

As we have seen, the Great Commandment consists of two parts: Love God with all your heart, soul, mind, and strength; and love your neighbor as you love yourself.

Pfftt. Like *those* are so hard to do, right? You could probably do them while sitting right there in your chair!

Let's *all* fulfill the Great Commandment, right now! Let's close our eyes, and love God with all our heart, soul, mind, and strength.

Ahhhhhh.

Feel your love for God.

Ahhhhhh.

Feel your love for your neighbor. Feel yourself feeling how he isn't really such a bad guy. Forget about how he constantly plays his stereo at concert-decibel levels, and how he seems convinced that his leaf blower endows him with a divine right to wake up the neighborhood at seven on a Saturday morning as he blows debris from his yard into everyone else's. Feel yourself forgetting how he flicks his cigarette butts over his fence onto your grass.

Don't you just *hate* your stupid, lazy, inconsiderate jerk of a neighbor?!

God is fine—but that guy! Who could love *that* guy?

Or the lady in the truck who cut you off on the freeway yesterday.

Or the coworker who keeps trying to take credit for your accomplishments.

Or the teacher whose imperviousness leaves her incapable of normal human interaction.

Or this person.

Or that person.

Or these people. Or those.

Now we begin to sense some of the more challenging aspects of the practical, everyday application of Jesus' supreme mandate.

Jesus sure knows how to pick his commandments.

Fundamentally, though, the Great Commandment really *is* pretty simple to execute. First, you love God. But you must love God seriously—with, in fact, all your heart, soul, mind, and strength. In order to fulfill the Great Commandment, you must get alone, take some time, and really, *really* love God.

And when you do that (in fact, *do* do that, right now), what happens?

What happens is the part of the Great Commandment that Jesus, in his awesome wisdom, left *out* so that we could discover it for ourselves.

What happens when you love God is that you feel how much God loves you.

That's the whole deal. That's how loving God works. (And you get a lot more love back from God than you give to him, too. You send your broken-up, scattered, can't-quite-focus, human sort of love up to him—and in return you receive this incredible, perfect, unmistakably divine love filling your every cell. It's like trading pennies for diamonds.)

First you love God, and then you're filled with God's love.

Then—and only then, only when you're filled with God's love—are you properly prepared to love even a neighbor as obnoxious as yours.

You can't love your neighbor with your normal, everyday, quick-to-anger, reactively judgmental, habitually evaluative mind. If you're really going to feel peaceful, benevolent, patient, and truly loving toward people—toward *all* people—then you're going to need undiluted, pure, direct-from-the-source divine Love.

You're going to need the love of God.

Which you can get one way, and one way only: by loving God.

In effect, the way to "do" the Great Commandment is to do only the first part of it. Once you've done that—once you've loved God with everything you are and have—the next part of it will happen automatically.

> Dear friends, let us love one another, for love comes from God. Everyone who loves has been born of God and knows God. Whoever does not love does not know God, because God is love. This is how God showed his love among us: He sent his one and only Son into the world that we might live through him. This is love: not that we loved God, but that he loved us and sent his Son as an atoning sacrifice for our sins. Dear friends, since God so loved us, we also ought to love one another. (1 John 4:7–11)

There are a lot of "one anothers" in the Bible, and if you look closely at them you get the impression that God expects us to be hanging around with, helping, encouraging, confronting, and in all cases loving one another. When you think about it, it seems impossible.

How can I possibly live up to the standard prescribed in the Great Commandment?

This is a very good question, because it points to the idea that the Great Commandment isn't as simple a directive as (God knows) so many Christians routinely assume it to be.

The answer is that you *can't* live up to the Great Commandment standard. No one can. You might be able to love God with all your heart, soul, mind, and strength for . . . what . . . two minutes at a time? Three? Five? A half hour, if you're, like, a monk? But sooner or later even a monk gets hungry and has to think about eating, or itches and has to think about scratching, or just gets a call on his BlackBerry. And sooner or later something will bring you, too, back to the big, bad world where, after all, your attention is necessary in order for you to live and make your way.

You simply cannot love God all the time in the kind of all-consuming way prescribed by this commandment. Not if you ever want to, say, order off a menu, much less operate heavy machinery. Likewise, you could no sooner consistently love every person in the world than you could open your mouth, dive into the sea, and suck up all the plankton. It's just not going to happen.

God knows that. He knows you can't ceaselessly love him and/or others with all the passion you possess. God knows—and a great deal better than any of us know it about ourselves—what our capacities are for giving and receiving love.

He knows we're human.

You know what God wants when it comes to our fulfilling the Great Commandment? He wants us to try. He wants us to consciously and purposefully love him as much and as often as we're able, and he wants us to be generous and loving toward our neighbors as often as we can possibly arrange it within ourselves to be so.

And when we fail to love God as much as we could, and when we fail to love our neighbor as much as we love ourselves, he wants us to ask him to forgive us for transgressing.

And why does God want us to ask him for his forgiveness?

Because he wants us to again be filled with the fullness of his love for us.

And *that*—life-giving, heart-healing, joy-restoring, courage-rendering cycle—is what living as a Christian is all about.

It's not really about perfectly fulfilling the Great Commandment. It's about the learning and the loving that comes from continuously trying to.

God, who said, "Let light shine out of darkness," made his light shine in our hearts to give us the light of the knowledge of the glory of God in the face of Christ.
(2 Corinthians 4:6)

So don't forget that when you're out there being who you are and doing your best to shine for God, sometimes the shine is going to come off. God knows that. Hey, everybody's human. But don't let a mistake become a pattern or a habit. Hit the Life Reboot key, seek forgiveness, and move on. Because moving on is exactly where God wants you: moving on and out into the world to do something extraordinarily great.

What is the Great Commission— and what makes it so great?

The Great Commission is the term Christians have traditionally used to refer to something Jesus said to his disciples after he'd come back to life following the crucifixion. (See the

Question, "Why is Christ's resurrection so important to me?" on page 126.)

When people talk about this commission, they're usually referring to its most familiar version, found in the gospel of Matthew (28:16–20):

> Then the eleven disciples went to Galilee, to the
> mountain where Jesus had told them to go. When they
> saw him, they worshiped him; but some doubted. Then
> Jesus came to them and said, "All authority in heaven
> and on earth has been given to me. *Therefore go and
> make disciples of all nations, baptizing them in the name
> of the Father and of the Son and of the Holy Spirit, and
> teaching them to obey everything I have commanded
> you.* And surely I am with you always, to the very end of
> the age" (emphasis ours).

The italicized sentence is the commission's very core. What makes the Great Commission so monumentally important in the history and future of Christianity is the degree to which believers have always understood it as a spur to evangelize—that is, as an inspiration to them *personally* to try their best to help nonbelievers see, understand, and accept the supremacy of Jesus in their lives.

Anyone who's ever come up to you and said anything like "Have you heard the Word of the Lord?" or "Have you accepted Jesus Christ as your personal Lord and Savior?" was doing their best to fulfill this commission.

> You will receive power when the Holy Spirit comes on
> you; and you will be my witnesses in Jerusalem, and
> in all Judea and Samaria, and to the ends of the earth.
> (Acts 1:8)

Then he said to his disciples, "The harvest is plentiful but the workers are few. Ask the Lord of the harvest, therefore, to send out workers into his harvest field" (Matthew 9:37–38).

Actually, this book is our attempt to fulfill the Great Commission through reaching out and teaching. We like doing it this way. But of course there are many different ways to go about doing the same thing, and not everyone is expected to do it the way anyone or everyone else does.

Do I need to evangelize the nonbelievers in my life?

No, you certainly don't "need" to evangelize. You can rest assured that God is perfectly capable of bringing people to himself in his own good time and in his own good way. That said, though, it's very likely you *will* be galvanized by your own joy in the Lord to share that joy with others. It's only natural to want to share something wonderful you've found with everyone around you—and *especially* with those in your life for whom you have affection or care about. And if that life-enhancing, life-saving something you've found is absolutely *free* to anyone who will but ask for it, well . . . well then it's a wonder, isn't it, that every Bible sold doesn't come with a bullhorn.

The question of exactly when and how it's best for you to personally share your faith with others is one that the Holy Spirit stands ever ready to help you answer. Primarily, it's a matter of simply paying attention to the signals you get from non-Christians about the degree to which they're ready to have a conversation in which it would be natural to talk about the value and nature of personal beliefs. Forcing that conversation is unlikely to prove productive to you or to the other person. You don't want to alienate someone by too zealously pushing

Christ on them before they're open to that sort of interaction with you.

The best rule of thumb when wondering how and when you should go about evangelizing is to *just be yourself, and relax about it.* When it's time to talk to someone about Jesus, Jesus by his Spirit will let you know. Trust in this. God's ultimate purpose is to bring every person on earth to the realization that his Son died so they might have eternal life. And as a Christian you *do* have a role in that inspiring mission. Trust God to let you know when it's time for you to step into it—how, and with whom.

> You yourselves are our letter, written on our hearts, known and read by everybody. You show that you are a letter from Christ, the result of our ministry, written not with ink but with the Spirit of the living God, not on tablets of stone but on tablets of human hearts. (2 Corinthians 3:2–3)

> You are the light of the world. A city on a hill cannot be hidden. Neither do people light a lamp and put it under a bowl. Instead they put it on its stand, and it gives light to everyone in the house. In the same way, let your light shine before men, that they may see your good deeds and praise your Father in heaven. (Matthew 5:14–16)

> In your hearts set apart Christ as Lord. Always be prepared to give an answer to everyone who asks you to give the reason for the hope that you have. But do this with gentleness and respect. (1 Peter 3:15)

Francis of Assisi, a medieval mendicant monk and an all-around amazing guy, once said that we ought to tell everyone we meet about God—and, if we have to, as a last resort, use words. Pretty cool, huh? I really like the attitude of Father Francis.

What should my attitude be toward the nonbelievers in my life?

Your attitude toward everyone should be marked by love, patience, good humor, and understanding—and that should *certainly* be your attitude toward nonbelievers, who might, after all, be looking to you as a source of help in determining how they feel about faith in Jesus.

As a new Christian, you may find yourself feeling the way converts quite often do, which is filled with the desire to share their newfound faith. (Refer to the previous Question, "Do I need to evangelize the nonbelievers in my life?" on page 76.) That's a beautiful and honorable impulse: Once again, what kind of person *doesn't* want to share with others something infinitely wonderful they've discovered? It makes sense if, having recently been saved, you feel yourself welling with desire to share the gospel's very good news.

What sometimes happens, though, is that the zeal to share this newfound relationship with Jesus morphs into a drive to convert others. And the transition from "I'm saved!" to "You need to be saved!" may not be much of a "morph" at all: Oftentimes new converts to our glorious faith are told by the Christians around them that trying to bring nonbelievers to a Jesus-commitment— that doing one's utmost to carry out the Great Commission—is *the* very mark of a true believer. (Look again at the Question, "What is the Great Commission—and what makes it so great?" on page 74.)

New converts are, by nature, the most zealous evangelizers of all.

If it's your impulse to be an evangelist—if you're energized to get out there and try to awaken nonbelievers to the wondrous, living miracle you've discovered—and if that's what the Christians in your life are encouraging you to do—then by all means, buy the biggest bullhorn you can find. Far be it from us to put a damper on anything you hear the Holy Spirit telling you.

Do, though, allow us to offer this one truism: When talking to a nonbeliever about your relationship with Jesus, you can never go wrong talking about—or at least making sure you include talking about—what that relationship means to you *personally*.

People are generally amenable to hearing, "This is why Christianity works for *me*." What most people are not generally amenable to hearing—not right off the bat, or out of nowhere, and definitely not if they aren't on intimate terms with you—is, "This is why Christianity will work for *you*."

Tell me how you've changed, and how that change has improved your life, and I'm pretty guaranteed to be interested.

Tell me how *I* should change, and how that change will improve *my* life, and I'm pretty guaranteed to find myself a new lunch partner.

The bottom line is that when it comes to dealing with nonbelievers generally—and *particularly* when it comes to the issue of trying to convert them—always take care to heed the inner voice of the Spirit. God inside you will tell you how to interact.

If there's one thing in this world you can count on, it's that Jesus, the Prince of Peace, really does know a thing or two about peace. And to whatever extent it's possible, peace *is* what you want between yourself and every other person in your life. Because as we have seen, Christ explicitly commanded all his followers to love their neighbors as they love themselves. (See the Question, "What is the Great Commandment—and what makes it so great?" on page 69.) And you can't have a loving relationship with someone you've alienated; you can't, in other words, have a loving relationship with someone with whom you have no relationship at all.

So if you're feeling compelled to evangelize, consider the validity of balancing that compulsion with your innate ability to be diplomatic and respectful. Take your time. Find the balance that works best between you and the people you most yearn to engage.

Listen to the Prince of Peace when he tells you where that balance lies.

> [God] has committed to us the message of reconciliation.
> We are therefore Christ's ambassadors, as though God
> were making his appeal through us. (2 Corinthians
> 5:19–20)

Quite frankly, it also might be a very good idea to be sure you're solidly grounded in the faith before you become an "expert" who is trying to convey it to others. Getting your new life separate from your old one is the first order of business.

Once I'm saved, how definite must the break be between my old life and my new life?

It depends, of course, on the quality of your old life. If you were a crack-smoking bank robber, then it's safe to say becoming a Christian would mean a pretty radical lifestyle change. If you already were a kind person who'd been going to church for a year with your best friend, that break would probably look somewhat different.

The important thing is to listen to the Holy Spirit, who will inwardly direct you toward those things that encourage the deepening of your relationship with God, and away from those things that hinder it. Let the Spirit be your guide, and your step will always be true.

What you do want to be aware of, though, is the tendency some novice Christians have of too dramatically severing their "new" friends from their old. Sometimes, when people convert, they get so thrilled about the newness of their lives that they hasten to cut off anything and anybody they feel is, in a sense, "unclean"—anyone who doesn't fit with their immediate understanding of the new person they've become. And in that rush, they sometimes end up throwing out the baby with the bathwater.

Back before John became a Christian, for instance, he had a friend named Norm. Though not a believer, Norm sometimes went to church with a Christian friend of his, and in general he enjoyed participating in a lot of that church's activities: cookouts, game nights, etc.

One time Norm went on a four-day camping retreat with a bunch of folks from his friend's church. When he returned, he was as Christian as Christian gets! He'd been saved! He'd found the Lord!

Hallelujah!

John was genuinely happy for Norm. He could see how happy being saved made Norm; he'd known that this was a place to which Norm had been gravitating for a while. He was pleased by this happy culmination of his friend's personal spiritual quest.

Except, guess what? Norm didn't want anything to do with John anymore. He came home, declared his faith, and asked John if he wanted to be saved. When John demurred, Norm summarily dropped him from his life.

And this sort of thing is understandable. One of the things Norm learned at the retreat where he'd been saved—and one that converts are often taught—is that part of being a new Christian is instantly cleansing from your life anything and anyone that doesn't directly enhance or improve your relationship with Christ. So Norm got rid of all his "satanic" rock albums, threw away all his "un-Christian" books, removed from his walls any "worldly" pictures—and stopped answering or returning John's calls.

This hurt John's feelings; he and Norm had, after all, been good friends. And John actually wanted to know more about the change Norm had undergone—but Norm's refusal to socialize with him meant he couldn't learn about that change firsthand.

Not good. But this story later returned to happy chapters: Norm and John have since become friends again; Norm apologized, and John got something he could use to emotionally blackmail Norm into buying him lunch. So everyone was pleased.

While endeavoring to rid yourself of anything detrimental to your growing relationship with Christ, you also want to avoid doing what Norm did, which is to put yourself in a position of later having to buy lunch for someone whenever they opt to play that card.

Because they *will* play that card.

And they *will* want a side of onion rings.

Trust us on this.

The point is: When you're a new Christian, use your better judgment about what things and people do and don't fit into your new life. Ask God to help direct you in each and every one of those calls. He will. If you listen to him, he will let you know *exactly* how to shape your new life with him.

Do not conform any longer to the pattern of this world,
but be transformed by the renewing of your mind. Then
you will be able to test and approve what God's will
is—his good, pleasing and perfect will. (Romans 12:2)

Remember: The transformation comes from renewing your mind with the truth you may have ignored for a long time. Transformation does not come from running everybody off that cares about you just because they knew you BBC. (See the Question, "To what do the words *born again* actually refer?" on page 32.) Refuse to be with those who are a very negative influence, but be kind to them. And if you're married to someone like that, well, that's a different story.

What if my spouse or a family member isn't Christian?

Many, if not most, believers have at least one family member who doesn't share their faith. The thing to remember is that there are in essence three components involved in any relationship you have with another person: You, the other person, and the unique relationship that exists between the two of you. That's all of it, right there: That's the whole Relationship Combo. You handle correctly each of those three aspects of every relationship you have, and each of those relationships will come out all right.

So the question is, what attitude—what guiding principle, what constantly motivating emotional truth—should you take care to bring to each of those three dimensions in your relationship with a nonbeliever, and especially with one who's a family member?

About yourself, be humble.

Toward the other person, be loving.

Toward the relationship between the two of you, be patient.

Humility, love, and patience. There is no mountain these three can't move.

Let's take a quick look at each.

Humility

You must keep your awareness of this quality at the fore of your consciousness whenever you're dealing with a nonbeliever you're close to. Failing to do so is likely to result in your demeanor becoming strident: You will (however subtly) begin preaching, lecturing, telling them what, how, and who they should be. That's not the sort of oil that keeps the wheels of a relationship spinning smoothly.

We all know we must be humble before God. Let us also not forget to be humble before the people in our lives—each one of whom is, after all, an illustration of God's greatest creation, and made in his image. Remember: You didn't *deserve* to be saved. Being chosen by God isn't anything to be proud of. It's something to be grateful for.

Love

As God loves us, we must love others. Of course, this can be difficult—just look at what it cost Christ to unconditionally and absolutely love us. If our Lord can suffer that, we can suffer whatever psychological or emotional pain it causes us to remain loving toward someone—and especially toward any nonbeliever, for whom we can trust that God has an acute interest.

God counts on us to love others, to be his loving agents on earth. Simply *love* the nonbeliever in your life. Christ will take it from there.

Patience

This is God's world, not ours. *We* keep time; we have watches and calendars and clocks and so on. God sits at the heart of eternity. You can bet on this: He's not wearing a wristwatch. When it comes to the relationship between you and a nonbeliever—and particularly a nonbeliever to whom you're necessarily close—be patient. Wait. *Never stop waiting.* Have no agenda. Let God's will, in God's time, shape the relationship.

When you're involved with a nonbeliever, you're involved in one of the most important, precious dynamics given to any believer. Don't try to start driving that relationship in the way *you* think it should go. Give God the wheel. All you have to do with your nonbeliever friend is climb into the backseat with them—and then, side by side, relaxing and looking out the window, the two of you can enjoy the ride together.

The fruit of the Spirit is love, joy, peace, patience,
kindness, goodness, faithfulness, gentleness and self-

control. Against such things there is no law. (Galatians 5:22–23)

Live such good lives among the pagans that, though they accuse you of doing wrong, they may see your good deeds and glorify God on the day he visits us. (1 Peter 2:12)

Of course, sometimes people aren't happy to let you be you, while they are who they are. Sometimes people throw hostility (and more) your way just because you're a Christian.

How do I respond to others attacking my newfound faith in Christ?

It depends. If someone is being virulent to you about Christianity, the best thing to do is politely walk away. It's usually not helpful or productive to try to thoughtfully or rationally engage such a person. As the inimitable British playwright George Bernard Shaw wrote, "Never wrestle with a pig. You get dirty; and besides, the pig likes it."

Not that the person denigrating Jesus is a pig.

Still, what kind of person makes a point of maligning the faith of another? That really *is* a pretty . . . oinky thing to do.

Interesting, isn't it, how some people seem to focus—not to say obsess—on the idea that Christianity is something against which they personally, fervently, and usually quite vocally need to react? It's not hard to imagine that what such people actually want is to engage in an honest and open conversation about the faith; why poke a bear with a stick if you truly have no interest in the bear? So to the extent you find it feasible or possible, always remain open to the possibility that what the person who seems to hate Christianity might be responding against is an inextricable (and perhaps even subconscious) pull toward the very object of their disdain.

Bottom line: If it's someone you don't know who's attacking your faith, exit gracefully—but exit, and don't look back. If it's an acquaintance you're basically or conditionally stuck with for a while—a coworker, a classmate, that sort of person—then be patient, and polite, and if they grow too offensive, ask them to please stop speaking to you as they are, to please have the same respect for your belief system that you have for theirs. (And do ask them to talk to you about their beliefs! Start a dialogue!) Always, in both cases, remain open to the possibility, no matter how apparently small, that at some level all the other person really wants is to just *talk* about Jesus.

Maybe a little martial-arts principle would help. Rather than knock heads, go with the attacker's momentum and enjoy the engagement. And turn it into a practiced, developed skill. The truth is, there always will be people who are either going to be mean to you or do mean things to you. And once they do, you have a new responsibility to get over it rather than live under it.

Does being a Christian mean I have to forgive everyone who's ever done anything bad to me?

There are two modes of consciousness possible for believers: Christ consciousness, and . . . *me* consciousness—that is, our everyday, normal, human, self-focused sort of consciousness.

When we're filled with Christ consciousness—when we're fully with God, fully open to Christ, fully imbued with the Spirit's power—we cannot help but forgive anyone for anything. To be filled with Christ consciousness is to be filled with love, and pure love forgives as easily as scent comes off a rose. Modeling this cause-and-effect we have, of course, Jesus himself, who unforgettably proclaimed his forgiveness for his killers even as they delightedly crowed at his suffering. ("Father, forgive them, for they do not know what they are doing" [Luke 23:34].) *That* shows the power of Christian forgiveness.

And it's important that we learn to forgive like this, because it's important that as often as possible we ask the Lord to fill us with his Holy Spirit.

But most of us aren't usually so overflowing with the Spirit that if we got mugged we'd be swimming in thoughts of how much we love and forgive the criminal as he busily clubs us about the head. We're just not geared toward that level of forgiveness. In fact, most of us can't instantly forgive someone who budges into the "10 Items or Less" aisle with eleven items in their cart!

We have our spiritual, Christ-filled mode of consciousness, and we have our material, self-identification mode of consciousness.

The Spirit of God, and the mind of . . . us. It's the ongoing mixing, experiencing, and juxtaposing of the two that describes and defines the internal life of all Christians.

If with our *human* mind we attempt to forgive a grievous offense, we're almost certain to fail; resentment (however deep it's buried) is sure to linger. And even if we try to forgive such an offense by bringing it into the realm of our Christ consciousness, we will invariably find ourselves still pained by it once we've reassumed that mode of consciousness by which we must, after all, tend to the practical, everyday business of life.

Because we live as humans, we must (also) forgive as humans.

And what *that* means is not only must we forgive in the absolute, spiritual, Jesus-focused sense that our heart can understand, we must also forgive in the relative, material, human-centered sense that our mind can understand.

Let's take a real-life example. When John was eight years old his mother and father divorced, and his father moved away from home. Two years later, when John was ten, his mother suddenly disappeared on him and his sister. She said she was going to leave the house for a few minutes to go pick up some things from the grocery store down the street. She got into her car, drove away, and then she *stayed* away for two years.

Not once during those two years did John's mother in any way contact him or his sister. They didn't know if she had been kidnapped, or killed, or abducted by aliens, or what. (It turned out she had wanted the time away in order to come to terms with the fact that, as she put it upon her return, "God never intended me to be a mother.")

Well, for John, it's not just about, in the absolute spiritual sense, "forgiving" his mother for her two-year absence, because the damage caused by her abandonment was too visceral—too emotionally violent, too grounded in the child he was at the time—to be assuaged purely through the mechanism of spiritual "forgiveness."

In a vital sense, what happened to John is not strictly a matter of spiritual concern. It's also very much a matter of emotional concern.

Before John can "forgive" his mother for what she did when he was ten, he must first *understand* what she did. He must consciously come to terms with the how's and why's of the path she chose for herself. He can't short-circuit or end-around the very real and difficult mental and psychological work—the *human* work—that he must go through in order to finally come to where he's able to spiritually forgive his mother.

(John has, by the way, both spiritually and intellectually—with his heart *and* with his mind—forgiven his mother. With his Christian eyes he sees her in the light of Christ's love, and with his human eyes he sees her as someone who, those many years ago, was struggling with issues of her own. He understands that everyone struggles with personal issues; why should his mother be different?)

So the answer to whether being a Christian means you have to forgive everyone who's ever done anything unloving to you is: Yes, you must forgive others their trespasses against you, *as God forgives your trespasses against him.* But achieving absolute and lasting forgiveness for any real offense against you is going to take more than the all-covering, divinely inspired forgiveness that flows forth with the attainment of Christ consciousness. Besides your redeemed heart, true forgiveness also requires your still-being-renewed mind. Both have a definite role to play in the process that culminates in true forgiveness.

Sometimes to forgive someone, all you have to do is take a moment to understand them—to walk a mile in their shoes. Sometimes you can look at the person who doesn't belong in the "10 Items or Less" aisle and simply accept that something difficult must be going on with them. Maybe they're too old to adequately consider exactly how many items they're buying. Maybe just then—or maybe permanently—they're too emotionally tweaked to handle that kind of specificity. Maybe they're in a hurry because they have someone sick at home. You don't know. Half the time knowing that you *don't* understand someone is all the understanding you need to feel peace and forgiveness toward them.

Other times, knowing that you really aren't aware of what caused another person to act the way they did means you've got to roll up your mental sleeves, dig into your emotional and psychological warehouse, and keep working in there until you can put together and then bring out into the light a full and true comprehension of what happened.

Yes, we all need to use the power of Christ to forgive others.

But we've also got to remember that, just as Christ fully engaged his humanity as a means of understanding ours, we must engage our humanity as a means of understanding others.

There is neither Jew nor Greek, slave nor free, male nor
female, for you are all one in Christ Jesus. (Galatians 3:28)

Peter came to Jesus and asked, "Lord, how many times
shall I forgive my brother when he sins against me? Up to
seven times?" Jesus answered, "I tell you, not seven times,
but seventy-seven times" (Matthew 18:21–22).

Let us finish this off by saying that the most dangerous thing
anyone can carry around is a "justifiable resentment." If you're
"justified" because the person who hurt you was so cruel, you
may be tempted to live in bitterness, deteriorating your own life.
Nope, there's only one really good choice and that is to begin the
process of forgiveness. Then one day you may find yourself even
wanting good things for that person . . . even actively praying for
those good things to happen.

Do I have to pray for my enemies?

Once more, you don't *have* to do anything—though you should
know that if you don't pray for your enemies you'll be flagrantly
disregarding God's specific directions and will go straight to hell
the second you die.

But, you know: It's up to you.

Totally kidding. Seriously, now: Yes, if there's *anyone* in
this world for whom you really should make a point of praying,
it's your enemies. Now, that doesn't mean you're expected to
immediately start praying for good things to drop on someone
who's betrayed you or hurt you or taken something valuable
from you. It's natural to be angry at someone who does you
wrong. But when you work through that anger, you come to
where you're able to pray for your enemies. That doesn't let
them off the hook with God, but it benefits you greatly. Here
are some reasons why.

(1) *Jesus really did tell you to do this.*

In Matthew 5:44, Jesus says, "Love your enemies and pray for those who persecute you." And in Luke 6:27–28 he says, "Love your enemies, do good to those who hate you, bless those who curse you, pray for those who mistreat you." So there it is.

(2) *You are to do to others as you'd have them do to you.*

"In everything, do to others what you would have them do to you, for this sums up the Law and the Prophets" (Matthew 7:12). Obviously, we'd rather someone pray for our well-being than pray for our . . . well, for the sorts of things we tend to wish upon our enemies during our less charitable moments.

(3) *Prayer greatly enhances your understanding of the situation between you and your "enemy."*

For reasons and in ways we mortals will never understand, prayer creates miracles. One of these is emotional and mental clarity on the part of the one praying. If ever we're in need of such clarity, it's when we're suffering through the stress related to conflict. Praying for your enemies—specifically praying that good things happen to them, that they prosper, that (if they're not already) they get saved—brings you this clarity. It's a priceless thing to have when you're all tangled up in knots over someone you're at odds with.

(4) *Prayer relieves stress.*

This one's connected to the above. As these days everyone knows, stress is positively lethal. Being filled with rage is one of the most stressful things you can do to your body. *Really* want to irk someone you're in conflict with? Pray for their health and well-being. You'll end up being healthier, and you'll live longer. *That'll* show 'em!

(5) You want to be a good example of Christianity.

Anyone can have a great personality when things are going well. It's when things go sour that who a person really is truly shows. Remember that if you're a Christian, you're not out in the world simply representing yourself. You're also—and even primarily—out in the world as a representative of Jesus Christ. Nonbelievers—and especially nonbelievers with whom you have disagreements—*will* notice every measure of discrepancy between your professed values and what you actually do and say. Praying for your enemy allows the Holy Spirit to figure into your relations with the person you're praying for, which then allows you to behave toward that person in a way that will mark you as someone they can at least respect. More important, it marks you as someone Jesus is proud to have representing him here on earth. The way *not* to let Christ down is to pray for your enemies.

> Bear with each other and forgive whatever grievances
> you may have against one another. Forgive as the Lord
> forgave you. And over all these virtues put on love, which
> binds them all together in perfect unity. Let the peace of
> Christ rule in your hearts, since as members of one body
> you were called to peace. And be thankful. (Colossians
> 3:13–15)

> When you stand praying, if you hold anything against
> anyone, forgive him, so that your Father in heaven may
> forgive you your sins. (Mark 11:25)

You just can't lose when you work through justifiable resentment and move into forgiveness, freeing yourself from experiencing the hurt over and over again. And it's also a great way to begin increasing your compassion for others.

How can I increase my compassion for other people?

The best way is to really, really listen to them. Listen to their pain, watch for their discomfort, become aware of the little signs they're constantly giving off that they're unsure, afraid, confused, defeated. Allow your love, empathy, and compassion to be triggered by those signals. Let your heart feel the fullness of their suffering.

Contrarily, an outstanding way to develop compassion for others is to observe how strong they are, how valorous, how brave, how confident, how loving, how much fun.

There isn't a person in this world who within a minute of your being with them, won't do or say something for which you can genuinely love them. The way they smile. The way they're polite to a waiter or an attendant. The way they keep everything so clean and neat—or the way they don't. Just the regular, everyday stuff about the way people live can be profoundly endearing. All you have to do is watch for it. Noting the unique, careful way they have of taking care of and going about their business is one of the best things about hanging out with people.

People *are* lovable, and we are designed to love our own kind. Go with that. Open yourself up to the truth that every man and woman really is your brother and sister.

Finally, develop the practice of viewing people not through your eyes, but through the eyes of God within you. None of us— what with our actually being human, and all—can help but to some degree see others in terms relative to ourselves. We wonder: Is this or that person better looking than we are? Are they more successful, happier, smarter, more powerful than we are? Making that kind of relative evaluation is a human instinct. It's part of what people do when they interact with or observe others. Well, try your best to *stop* doing it. Or at least try to *sometimes* stop doing it. And the only way to do that is to let go, and let God. (See the Question, "What's the best thing to constantly tell myself in order to always remember my true and proper relationship to God?" on page 39.)

We normally see people in relative terms. God sees them in only one way: with love.

With the help of the Holy Spirit, we can see them that way, too.

> As God's chosen people, holy and dearly loved, clothe
> yourselves with compassion, kindness, humility, gentleness
> and patience. (Colossians 3:12)

Most of us are familiar with the Nike slogan, "Just Do It." The reason I like it is that we're called to do a lot of things we don't enjoy, things we don't feel like doing but have to do anyway. Don't try to get too philosophical about compassion. Start handing it out, even when you don't feel like it, and it will begin to saturate your life; it will become part of who you are and how you act toward others.

Is part of being a Christian having to act toward others with more kindness than I actually feel toward them?

It'd be great if we could tell you that being a Christian doesn't have anything to do with how you treat other people—but we'd be lying. The answer is yes: A Christian is always obliged (and should always be pleased) to treat everyone as . . . well, as they themselves would like to be treated. And since no one ever wants to be treated with anything but thoughtfulness, love, patience, and respect, then that's the way all of us who claim to follow

Jesus must learn to treat each person with whom we come in to contact every day.

Don't think of always having to treat people well as a way to end up with smoke pouring out your ears. Think of it as what it is: a profoundly important, eminently practical, and wildly challenging spiritual discipline.

And if *that* doesn't work for you, think of how you treat others as the clearest, surest, most reliable way the world has of measuring where you are as a Christian. Because *anyone* can complain, scream, accuse, criticize, take offense, and generally indulge in all manner of self-righteous indignation. Is there anything in the world easier (or, sadly, more natural) than behaving in that manner? The world is chockablock with angry, childish people who just *know* they're right about everything in the universe (even—and especially—when they're manifestly wrong). You get no prize for belonging to that entirely too-inclusive club.

But the man who by the strength of his character and the depth of his love consistently turns swords into plowshares? Well, *that* man is someone who pleases God, not to mention other people. Being consistently fair, good-spirited, and respectful in your dealings with others goes together with being a Christian the way bread and wine go together during the Lord's Supper. It's no small matter. We can pray, be pious, read our Bible every day, regularly swoon as we feel the Spirit opening up inside of us, but what in the end we'll be judged for—what will always stand as the full measure of our relationship with God—is how we treat other people.

> Accept one another, then, just as Christ accepted you, in order to bring praise to God. (Romans 15:7)

> If you show favoritism, you sin and are convicted by the law as lawbreakers. (James 2:9)

Then he [Jesus] will say to those on his left, "Depart from me, you who are cursed, into the eternal fire prepared for the devil and his angels. For I was hungry and you gave me nothing to eat, I was thirsty and you gave me nothing to drink, I was a stranger and you did not invite me in, I needed clothes and you did not clothe me, I was sick and in prison and you did not look after me."

They also will answer, "Lord, when did we see you hungry or thirsty or a stranger or needing clothes or sick or in prison, and did not help you?"

He will reply, "I tell you the truth, whatever you did not do for one of the least of these, you did not do for me."

"Then they will go away to eternal punishment, but the righteous to eternal life" (Matthew 25:41–46).

That passage from Matthew is usually used to illuminate the Christian imperative to serve the needy among us. We use it here, though, as a reminder that quite often, instead of feeling angry or impatient with difficult people, it's helpful if we consider them to be *suffering*. Because they are. It is, after all, when people are suffering—when they're in some sort of bad psychological place, or feeling threatened or confused or for whatever reason just aren't thinking straight—that they act selfishly, arrogantly, angrily, stupidly. People get crazy when they're scared, upset, lost. And no wonder: that's a bad place to be.

It's easy enough to give food to a hungry person. But we'd better understand that Christ also expects us to give spiritual food—in other words, treat them as we would wish to be treated—to people who are clearly suffering as much psychologically as others might be materially. Need is need. Our job is to call upon the Holy Spirit to help us serve everyone in any kind of need. Even when we don't feel like it.

How can I learn to act toward others with more kindness than I actually feel?

Practice. Get out in the world. Mix it up. Don't avoid potentially tough issues with someone because you sense or know that doing so might bring you into conflict with them. With a Spirit-filled heart and a mind attuned to God's will, go ahead and wade right in. See if you can't turn what might have been pain into pleasure.

Mostly, pray. Spend time with God. Make sure it's him *through* you that is engaging with the grizzly-bearish people in your life. Because it's an absolute truth that you, on your own, will fail in your quest to be patient, warm, and immediately forgiving of those who sometimes seem as if their entire life's purpose is to make sure that you go to jail for strangling them.

Dealing in a healthy, positive way with troublesome people—becoming, in that very real sense, superhuman—is all about calling upon God's Spirit.

And let us say it again: Pray. If there's someone you can't seem to come within two blocks of without practically breaking into hives, pray about that person. Pray *for* that person. (See the Question, "Do I have to pray for my enemies?" on page 90.)

Finally, consider the very real possibility that God brought that person into your life specifically to see how you would deal with them. Try to think of that person not as someone you'd like to leave behind on a desert island, but rather as a live-action, 3-D *test* set before you by Jesus Christ, the ultimate teacher.

> The fruit of the Spirit is love, joy, peace, patience,
> kindness, goodness, faithfulness, gentleness and self-
> control. (Galatians 5:22–23)

Now, it's really hard to get a pear from a cactus plant. I'm not saying it's not possible, or that it won't ever happen, but today that's still quite a challenge. By the same token, if you're sort of a cactus-like person, the fruit of kindness will be a challenge to get from you. So the best way to work on kindness is to work on your soul, your character, and being filled more and more with the Holy Spirit. Then increasingly you will yield and share the sweet fruit of kindness.

Is there such a thing as being too kind?

There's no such thing as being too kind—but there is such a thing as enabling for too long someone whose behavior either needs to stop altogether, or to at least stop happening in *your* life.

Possible to be too kind? No.

Possible to be a patsy? Yes.

The two aren't really connected. No one is ever being "kind" by continuing to in any way let another person victimize them or anyone else. It's a sad truth about this world that there are definitely people in it who, for whatever reason, are clearly determined to behave in ways detrimental to the psychological or physical well-being of those around them.

Treating someone as if they need to be accountable for their actions—insisting that they face the hard consequences of their behavior—isn't being unkind. It's actually treating them with respect. If someone's treating you poorly, and you let them continue to treat you poorly, what you're very clearly communicating is, "Good job. You *should* act abominably to me and to everyone around you. Because none of us, including you especially, has any honor, dignity, or self-respect at all. Of course we don't! We're all animals! Thank goodness you're always helping us to remember that!"

See? That's not a good message to send someone. No good can come of that.

But let's say you've tried your best and that you've applied all the faith and grace you have to bring a difficult person to the realization that for the good of themselves and everyone around them, they need to change. And let's say that they haven't changed, that the person in question continues to abuse your goodwill and best efforts.

There comes a time, when the only way you can continue doing that person any good is to say, in effect (though, come to think of it, do feel free to use these very words), "I give up. I can't change whatever it is that makes you do what you do. What I *can* do is stop letting you do what you do in my life. And that's what I'm doing, right now. That door right there leads into the rest of the world. I want you to go through it, close it firmly behind you, and see if you can't find yourself someplace where doing the stuff you do works for you. Because it definitely doesn't work for me. It breaks my heart to give up on you, but that's the choice I have to make. You and I both will have to live with it."

Now something like *that* might actually straighten a person out.

Either way, it's bound to do the person who says it some good.

God wants you to love others, of course. But he knows what, deep down in your heart, you also know. He knows that you can't love anyone the way you should until you love yourself the way you should. And sometimes loving yourself the way you should means no longer letting another person treat you as if you are anything less than a true child of the one true God.

He will reply, "I don't know you or where you come from. Away from me, all you evildoers!" (Luke 13:27).

Now back to that original question: Can you be too kind? Well, if your kindness is so "kind" that it enables evil to continue, then yes, that's too much kindness. But when we enable someone to do something that's hurting them, us, and/or others, that isn't really kindness at all. That's peacekeeping. Sounds admirable, yet in this context it's anything but. God doesn't honor those who wimp out in the name of kindness just to keep the peace. God honors those who make bold moves to make peace. And to be a peace*maker*, versus a peace*keeper*, you may have to do some things that on the surface may not seem kind but may in fact be the best medicine for a damaging person or a bad relationship.

What do I do if I'm in a bad relationship?

It depends on the nature of the relationship—and on how bad it really is. If you're being emotionally or physically abused, you may very well have to get out of that relationship. If, on the other hand, you're married, and your problem is that your spouse sometimes does stuff that basically annoys you, you may need to start being more realistic about what it takes to make a marriage work. It all depends.

The best advice for a Christian or anyone else in a bad relationship is the same: Be honest about that relationship, and communicate honestly about it. Be direct and upfront about how the relationship is making you feel, how it's affecting you psychologically, why you think it is that you're feeling and experiencing whatever things you are. Thoughtfully and thoroughly communicate all of this to the other person, taking care as you do so to be scrupulously honest about every last bit of it.

Honesty really is the best policy.

The challenge presented by being clear and honest with whomever you're sharing a bad relationship (especially if that relationship is longstanding and/or grounded in some real intimacy) is that it means you have to have *clarity* on whatever relational aspect has become difficult for you. You can't really communicate in plain, honest terms about something you're not clear on, in the same way you can't give a good description of a car you only glimpsed zipping by in the dark.

Honesty generally depends upon clarity—and mental and emotional clarity doesn't exactly go hand-in-hand with the kind of psychological and spiritual turmoil bad relationships tend to engender.

Oh, sure, in a difficult relationship you can (and, God knows, should) be honest about the fact that at times you're feeling confused or unclear. In just about any relationship you'll sometimes feel that way; for some people, this seems to be part of the appeal of remaining in a bad relationship. But, let's face it: During a time of strife, ambiguity can only take you so far. It's inevitable that sooner or later anyone in a bad relationship who doesn't decide for themselves how they want things resolved will have that question answered for them by the other person.

And you do *not* want to have someone else control what happens to you. Better to be driving a bus than get hit by a bus.

The bottom line is that relationships are like drinking water: the clearer, the better.

And being clear about who you are and what you want is where being a Christian really comes in handy. Because a dependable and utterly miraculous fact is that praying to Jesus for clarity actually brings clarity.

It's just . . . unbelievable.

But like so much of the unbelievable stuff God does every second of every day, it's also as true as true gets.

So (and if it sounds like this is our answer to way too many things, it's only because it *is* the answer for just about everything): pray.

If you're in a bad relationship, bring it before Jesus and ask him to put into your heart and mind what you should do about it. Don't anticipate God's answer to your plea; don't refute his answer; don't give up on him giving you an answer if within seconds of asking he doesn't give you a Ten-Point Relationship-Solving Plan that you can begin executing right away. Just remain faithful, and keep praying.

Trust that when asking for God's help, before long you *will* get that help. You'll know what to do. You'll know what to say. You'll know how to behave.

And then, of course, you'll have to actually *do* the things God has shown you to do. That's the other tricky part about being a Christian. We often hear, "Everyone who asks receives" (Luke 11:10). What we hear less often is "Don't ask if you don't want to receive."

Knowing what you should do is one thing. *Doing* what you know you should do is often a whole other kettle of slippery, wriggling fish.

Pray, and you'll know.

Know—and then take responsibility for knowing.

Not always easy, for sure. But since when is doing what's right always easy?

What every Christian in a bad relationship must recognize is no different from what every Christian must acknowledge: They belong to God. And that means they're precious to God. And that means they're doing him a severe disservice if they don't love and take care of themselves.

Stand firm then, with the belt of truth buckled around
your waist, with the breastplate of righteousness in
place, and with your feet fitted with the readiness that
comes from the gospel of peace. In addition to all
this, take up the shield of faith, with which you can
extinguish all the flaming arrows of the evil one. Take
the helmet of salvation and the sword of the Spirit,
which is the word of God. And pray in the Spirit on
all occasions with all kinds of prayers and requests.
(Ephesians 6:14–18)

Ever have a bad dog? I did. So I took him to a dog trainer. Man, did that dog become nice. I thanked the trainer for training my bad dog, and he told me something really shocking: He told me he hadn't trained the dog. He told me *I* had trained the dog to be bad. And the dog was under control *now* because the trainer had trained *me*.

So any of us in a bad relationship has to do what I had to do with a bad dog. We have to look at ourselves to see just how involved we've been in allowing or enabling the other person to do or say bad things to us. We may not be able to change the other person, but we can change ourselves—and sometimes that becomes great motivation for the other person to change as well. Either way, it's crucial that we work on ourselves rather than focus on the imperfections of anyone else. Because like it or not, all of us are going to make some pretty bad mistakes in any relationship.

How do I best understand, or deal with, "fallen" Christian leaders?

Well, if you're lucky enough to know a fallen leader of national prominence, the best thing to do is inflate, luridly embellish, and then sell whatever information you have to whatever media outlet offers you the most money for it.

And be sure not to forget some of the larger, more popular scandal-fueled Web sites, either—especially if you have a photograph showing the person whose life you're helping to ruin in any kind of compromising moment, or even just looking unfortunately stupid. Some of those sites nowadays offer the kind of money you used to have to go to *Geraldo* to get.

Sigh.

That's just what so many people seem to do, isn't it?

And heave a double sigh for our fallen Christian leaders. Will there be no end to their numbers?

The answer is no, there won't be. Why should there be? Christian leaders are people. They'll stop falling when we *all* stop falling. None of us should be blown away when a leader "falls." If anything, we should be surprised that it doesn't happen more often than it does.

Think about it: A Christian leader is someone who is in large part moral *for a living*. Being morally upright is a significant part of what they actually get *paid* to do.

Paul, in 1 Timothy 6:10, tells us that the love of money is a root of all kinds of evil. Big-time Christian leaders get crazy cash to publicly rebuke evil.

Can you imagine receiving mountains of money to proclaim that your true values have nothing whatsoever to do with money?

Talk about your delicate business plan. It really is a wonder that so very few of our most successful leaders fall.

Also, it's important to remember that becoming a media-friendly Big-Deal Christian takes a whole bunch of qualities that in and of themselves have nothing whatsoever to do with being an honorable man or woman of integrity. The Big-Dealer must be a fantastic public speaker, have a terrific memory, possess considerable ambition, and love being on camera. These rare and wonderful gifts are no more an indicator of character than "cute and furry" is an indicator of whether or not an animal will chomp your hand off. The two just aren't connected.

But they *seem* to be connected, no doubt. (Which is why every year vacationers to our national parks learn a terrible lesson about the difference between, say, Pooh Bear and a wild grizzly bear.) People are inclined to ascribe all kinds of wonderful and noble characteristics to a galvanizing, good-looking, funny, warm, confident, knowledgeable preacher holding ten thousand listeners in the palm of his hand. What's so easy to forget about someone charmingly transporting their audience is that what they're doing has a whole lot less to do with character than it does with show business.

Not that our leaders don't have countless valuable things to say to us. Of course they do. If they didn't, they wouldn't have made it to where so many people cared all that much if they fell. There's no question but that they're an asset to all of us. Besides, the good a person does isn't erased when he or she stumbles. If a man who from his own pocket has given millions to the poor later robs a liquor store, is the good he did the poor negated? Of course not. The good things we do remain forever. A man's sins don't cancel out the good he's done any more than fruit falling off a tree destroys that tree.

Every preacher who ever cracked open a Bible wants, just like the rest of us, to be loved for who they really and truly are. Not for what they do, or say, or think, or write. Not for how they look on TV. Not for how big their church is. Not for how many books they've gotten published. Not for what they represent. Not even because of their significance to a cause larger than themselves. They want to be loved for who they are.

Our Professionally Pious sometimes tumble from their towers for the same reason we all sometimes royally blow it in front of and all over the people whom we love most in the world, and whom we most want to love us.

They do it because they, too, yearn for confirmation that even at their worst they're still lovable.

What should your attitude be toward a fallen leader? The same as it should be for anyone who's crashed, who's fallen, or who's publicly humiliated themselves. You should feel compassion for them. You should hope everything turns out all right for them. You should pray that in their darkness they remember that they, too, already have what they want most, which is to be absolutely loved by him from whom all love flows.

And when one of our leaders messes up, *all* of us should take a moment to consider whether or not we ever contribute to the stress that leaders invariably feel to be superhuman. Do we insist, for instance, that the pastor of our own church is completely above temptation? Do we expect him to never lose his temper, never behave egotistically, never be judgmental? Because if we do, then we're contributing to the dynamic wherein sooner or later he, too, just might do something drastic in order to prove, once and for all, that he's only human.

All have sinned and fall short of the glory of God. (Romans 3:23)

Why do you look at the speck of sawdust in your brother's eye and pay no attention to the plank in your own eye? How can you say to your brother, "Brother, let me take the speck out of your eye," when you your- self fail to see the plank in your own eye? You hypocrite, first take the plank out of your eye, and then you will see clearly to remove the speck from your brother's eye. (Luke 6:41–42)

We know that in all things God works for the good of those who love him, who have been called according to his purpose. (Romans 8:28)

Even though God weaves things together to make good from what was meant to be evil, it hurts when someone you respect does something unrespectable. So be sure you grieve the loss of who you thought that person was. Grieve the loss of your ideal- ized image and accept that there is life after the fall, and you will recover from your sadness over what at the time might seem like a direct, personal betrayal. And of course, it's not just pastors for whom you have to do this; others a lot closer to you will get into trouble, and you will need to do the same for them.

How do I best understand,
or deal with, "fallen" fellow churchgoers?

It depends on what your relationship with them was before they fell. But generally speaking, love them. If it's appropriate to your relationship (and even if it's not, but *could* be), offer to spend time with them, to be with them, to listen to them. Show them what Christ's forgiveness looks like in immediate, mortal form.

John has a church friend we'll call Simon, who once went on a terrible drinking binge that lasted nearly a month and did substantial damage to his primary, personal, and professional relationships. When Simon quit drinking and realized the destruction he'd caused, he was devastated. One of the effects of having alienated himself from his own life was the feeling that he simply couldn't return to his church.

Another church friend of John's, Jim, stepped forward right away and unequivocally embraced Simon. He offered to meet with him once a week at the church for an hour's worth of chatting and some Scripture reading.

Every Tuesday, at one in the afternoon, Simon and Jim would sit in an empty Sunday school classroom in their church and just talk. And it was mostly Simon who talked; one of Jim's great gifts is that he's an extraordinarily empathetic listener.

That was ten years ago, and Simon (who hasn't had a drink since) says he will be forever grateful to the man who didn't abandon him when he was almost ready to abandon himself.

"As soon as I quit drinking, I began seeing a professional therapist," says Simon. "My therapy sessions weren't as valuable to me as my times with Jim. I felt so sheepish, especially around the church. I just didn't feel like I could ever belong there again. It was really helpful to actually be on the grounds with Jim, when no one else was around. It was such a good way to reintroduce me to a place I felt uncomfortable in. And in our meetings, Jim was always so completely nonjudgmental. He just listened and sympathized. And he never missed a Tuesday—not once—and this is a busy guy! I sure didn't miss any. Together, we read and studied the whole book of Job. Those months were one of the most healing periods of time I've ever experienced. I now look for opportunities to play in someone else's life the role that Jim played in mine."

That's a role we should all look to play in the life of someone who has stumbled.

As they say: United we stand.

Each one is tempted when, by his own evil desire, he is dragged away and enticed. Then, after desire has conceived, it gives birth to sin; and sin, when it is full-grown, gives birth to death. (James 1:14–15)

Be merciful, just as your Father is merciful. Do not judge, and you will not be judged. Do not condemn, and you will not be condemned. Forgive, and you will be forgiven. Give, and it will be given to you. A good measure, pressed down, shaken together and running over, will be poured into your lap. For with the measure you use, it will be measured to you. (Luke 6:36–38)

Like we said in the beginning, it's relationships that make life so very tough. But they also make life worth living. In your new life as a Christian, you're not going to get it very right all the time. But as you learn and grow and transform, your relationships will do the same thing, even in the midst of the ultimate downer we call sin.

CHAPTER THREE

Everyone:
Sin, the Human Constant

Let's jump right into this one, shall we?

What is sin?

Well, for starters, it's one of the most versatile words in the English language. It's a noun! ("Andy committed a sin when he purposefully ran that steamroller through the old folks' home.") It's a verb! ("Andy sinned when he took money from the collection plate.") It's an adjective! ("That Andy sure is sinful.") It's an adverb, even! ("Andy loves food that is sinfully delicious.")

But that's enough with the grammar lessons.

The point is, the word *sin* carries a lot of weight.

Most generally, of course, it's a noun: It's something a person does or thinks that's just plain ol' fashioned wrong. Within a Christian context, this means doing or thinking something that runs contrary to the loving will of God.

Classically—that is, within the context of old school, fire-and-brimstone-style Christianity (which, do let us say, we are in no way inclined to disparage: it does, after all, take strong roots to make strong trees)—a sin is understood as any act that violates one of God's laws. It's most particularly understood to be the violation of any of the Ten Commandments (see Exodus 20). Which of course makes sense: You violate one of The Big 10, and you've *definitely* done wrong. That's not just old school, of course; that's . . . forever school.

In an intensely individualistic, deeply personal way, a sin is anything you do that makes you feel guilty and foul. It's an act or even a thought that, however willfully or purposefully, removes you from the presence of God.

If after you do it you feel like something the cat dragged in, you've just sinned.

Which means you know *exactly* what a sin is—because if you're old enough to be reading this, you're old enough to have sinned so often in your life that the guilt of it all is probably eating away at you right this second! (Um. We're joking. But just in case: What Christians do when they're plagued with guilt is drop to their knees and implore God to forgive them their sins. Do it! He will! He *does!* That's the whole point!) Recognizing and suffering through the guilt and related effects caused by sin is as much a part of being human as is yawning when you're sleepy and scratching when you itch.

The truth is, anyone who asks what sin is, is kidding himself.

We *all* know what sin is.

Oh, God, do we ever.

Everyone who sins breaks the law; in fact, sin is
lawlessness. (1 John 3:4)

If we claim to be without sin, we deceive ourselves and
the truth is not in us. If we confess our sins, he is faithful

and just and will forgive us our sins and purify us from all unrighteousness. (1 John 1:8–9)

The point is that when you sin, the best reaction to it is godly sorrow. Guilt and shame keep us living back in the past where the mistakes were made. But godly sorrow motivates us to get our act together so that we can serve God and not embarrass him or turn away from him like the original sinners, Adam and Eve.

What is "original sin"?

Original sin is when you sin in a way that's so unique no one's ever sinned that way before. That's why it's original.

But we kid.

Seriously: We're kidding. Please don't actually *try* to find a new way to sin. Besides, it's not like you'd be able to. Without question, every way that it's possible for anyone to sin is a way people have been sinning since time began.

And why have people always sinned? Why is it impossible to be a human and *not* sin?

Because of the real meaning of "original sin."

The term usually refers to one of two things. The first is the *original* original sin—ground zero, as it were, for the whole *idea* of original sin. This is the actual event, recorded in the first book of the Bible (Genesis, chapter 3), when Adam and Eve, then blissfully living and gamboling about in the paradisiacal garden of Eden, ruined everything by shamelessly noshing on the one fruit God had very specifically told them not to ever, ever eat.

"Eat anything you want!" God (in effect) told the world's first couple. "Anything! The only thing I'm telling you not to eat is the fruit off this one tree, right here. *Don't eat that fruit* and everything'll be great."

111

So of course, that's the fruit Adam and Eve just had to gobble down.

And that's when everything, for everybody who would ever come after those two, started going straight to . . . well, You Know Where.

Curse that devil! (As you probably know, it was the silver-tongued Satan who sweet-talked Eve into taking that terrible first bite. We read in Genesis that he was "more crafty than any of the wild animals." Which makes us wonder how crafty animals used to *be,* anyway. Which is really beside the point, so never mind.)

So when people talk about original sin, they're often referring to the actual *first sin* ever committed by any human being.

The eating of the forbidden fruit in the garden is the original sin. Simple enough, right?

Usually, though, when people talk about original sin, they're referring to something a lot bigger and broader. They're usually referring to the *effect* of Adam and Eve's first transgression against the will of God, to the indelible stain of shame and sinfulness that their original sin made the legacy of all humanity after them.

Adam and Eve's first transgression against God precipitated this great and tragic Fall of Man. When through their willful disobedience they fell out of God's grace, we *all* fell out of God's grace. When those two got kicked out of the garden, it meant that for as long as we're in this life, *none* of us would ever be able to return to the state of blissful, constant communion with God that our Original Parents ruined by insisting *they* knew best what was good for them.

And so to this day we all struggle with the results—with the shame and the sinfulness—that come from those inevitable times when we, too, imagine we know what's better for us than God does.

Wanna see how angry God was at the audacity of Adam and Eve's disobedience, at the way they so clearly demonstrated that, in their opinion, the endless bounty he'd granted them just wasn't quite good enough?

Here's part of his response:

Then the Lord God said to the woman, "What is this you have done?"

The woman said, "The serpent deceived me, and I ate."

So the Lord God said to the serpent, "Because you have done this,

Cursed are you above all the livestock
and all the wild animals!
You will crawl on your belly
and you will eat dust
all the days of your life." . . .

To the woman he said,
"I will greatly increase your pains in childbearing;
with pain you will give birth to children.
Your desire will be for your husband,
and he will rule over you."

To Adam he said, " . . . Cursed is the ground because of you;

through painful toil you will eat of it
all the days of your life.
It will produce thorns and thistles for you,
and you will eat the plants of the field.
By the sweat of your brow
you will eat your food
until you return to the ground,
since from it you were taken;
for dust you are
and to dust you will return." . . .

So the Lord God banished him [Adam] from the Garden
of Eden to work the ground from which he had been
taken. After he drove the man out, he placed on the east
side of the Garden of Eden cherubim and a flaming sword
flashing back and forth to guard the way to the tree of life.
(Genesis 3:13–14, 16–19, 23–24)

Now that is one righteously ticked-off landlord executing the
eviction to end all evictions.

You know how you have to go to work every single morning, just so you can eat? You have Adam and Eve to thank for
that.

You know how you're forever feeling alienated from God's
grace as the result of your own sinful nature? You know the way,
in other words, that you, too, suffer from original sin?

You have Adam and Eve to thank for that.

You know how life can be such a struggle; how desperately
we all want to be loved; how selfish and greedy we are; how
easily we corrupt ourselves, how frail is our resolve to do and
be good?

You know how the whole human race just can't seem to ever
get enough of war?

You have Adam and Eve to thank for that.

Still we shouldn't be too hard on those erstwhile innocents.
They were, after all, only human.

Now the serpent was more crafty than any of the wild
animals the Lord God had made. He said to the woman,
"Did God really say, 'You must not eat from any tree in
the garden'?"

The woman said to the serpent, "We may eat fruit
from the trees in the garden, but God did say, 'You must
not eat fruit from the tree that is in the middle of the garden, and you must not touch it, or you will die.' "

"You will not surely die," the serpent said to the woman. "For God knows that when you eat of it your eyes will be opened, and you will be like God, knowing good and evil."

When the woman saw that the fruit of the tree was good for food and pleasing to the eye, and also desirable for gaining wisdom, she took some and ate it. She also gave some to her husband, who was with her, and he ate it. (Genesis 3:1–6)

The sinful nature desires what is contrary to the Spirit, and the Spirit what is contrary to the sinful nature. They are in conflict with each other, so that you do not do what you want. (Galatians 5:17)

Eden must have been an awfully nice place. But not nice enough for Adam and Eve to keep their act together. Some folks kind of think that when they become a Christian, the world should function for them just like it did in that botanical wonderland. Keep in mind that you are not back there; you are, instead, here. And because of the realities of here, it's going to be tough. You are going to be tempted; in one way or another, you are going to fall short; you are going to miss the mark, and sin.

Why is it important that Christians confess their sins?

Here's the deal with Christian confession: Being human, right off the bat, offers up some pretty significant challenges, yes? Premier among those challenges is the one constantly being taken up by all people, all the time: the will to be perfect.

We all want to be perfect. With all our heart, every single one of us yearns to be blameless, wonderful, superior, without guilt, generally inspirational, and absolutely sinless.

Especially absolutely sinless. That's really the state to which we all ultimately aspire.

Boy, do we wish we didn't sin.

But (surprise!) we do. It's in our nature to. (See the previous Question, "What is 'original sin'?" on page 111.) We could no sooner not sin than we could will ourselves to become invisible so that we could float around, where no one would ever be able to see us, so that we could . . . we could . . . well, never mind.

See?! We're such *sinners!*

Inevitably, we sin. And just as inevitably, after we sin we experience the jagged, harrowing affliction of guilt.

Curse that Adam and Eve! If it weren't for those miscreants, today we'd all be just as guilt-free as an apple hanging off a tree.

But, alas, that ain't us.

We sin.

And then we feel bad about it.

And then we feel driven to *do* something to relieve ourselves of our bad feeling.

And that, friend, is where the wondrous blessing of Christian confession comes in.

We have a great God. And one of the things that makes him so stunningly, inexpressibly great is that he cares so much about us. And the reason we know he cares so much about us is (for one) that he came down here, and he allowed himself to be slaughtered in order to establish for us a permanent, fail-proof means of absolutely cleansing ourselves of raw, grueling post-sin guilt.

Brothers and sisters! Let's get down on our knobby knees in gratitude for the relief our great God brings us from the severely caustic, destructive, and toxic emotion of guilt.

Guilt!

We cause it. We hate it. And confession is how we get absolved of it.

Relief of our guilt through confession of our sins to God is how we enter back into communion with him. We sin; we feel guilt; we drop to our knees; we pour our confession out to God; he forgives us our transgressions; in a natural outpouring of gratitude for that forgiveness—for that new lease on life we just got—we pledge to God to start representing him better than we have been; we rise; washed clean by the blood of Christ, and we go on. (See the Question, "What is the 'atonement' of Christ?" on page 121.)

And there, in a nutshell, is the Christian life.

If you're a new Christian, and you never learn anything else, learn to confess your sins to God.

If you don't know what a difference that makes, find out. Confess your sins to God. It'll change your life. Every blessed time.

The blood of Jesus, his Son, purifies us from all sin.
(1 John 1:7)

If we confess our sins, he is faithful and just and will
forgive us our sins and purify us from all unrighteousness.
(1 John 1:9)

In Him we have redemption through His blood, the
forgiveness of our trespasses, according to the riches of
His grace. (Ephesians 1:7, NASB)

If I do not wash you [of your sins], you have no part with
Me. (John 13:8, NASB)

Forgive us our sins, for we also forgive everyone who sins
against us. (Luke 11:4)

I can still remember the feeling of being a new Christian. It was just amazing. And then I sinned, and those feelings went away. But not forever. Because one sin does not destroy your salvation. What a relief that confessing to God can make all the difference in the world.

Why is repentance so important to me?

Because God can't hear you if you don't honestly and sincerely repent of your sins. (And repentance of your sins is, of course, part and parcel of confessing them. See the previous Question, "Why is it important that Christians confess their sins?" on page 115.)

Actually, God *can* hear you if you lie to him. But lying to God means profoundly shaming yourself—and when you willfully do that, God turns his face from you.

Bottom line? When you lie at all—but especially when you lie to God—you're on your own.

And if knowing full well that you've sinned, and you do not repent of your sin, then you have set yourself up as being opposed to God himself. Because by seeing no need to repent you have claimed your sin is justified.

By failing to seek forgiveness for your sin, you're saying you don't really need forgiveness. In effect, you've said that you can forgive yourself.

Worse yet: Implicit in failing to repent of your sins is the assertion that you're going to keep right on sinning.

And no matter how you cut it, that is *not* something you want to be communicating to God.

Look at what happens if, knowing you've sinned (and never kid yourself, you always know when you've sinned), you don't then repent of your sin: You lie to God; you shame yourself; you claim that what you did is okay; and you convey that you're going to keep on doing whatever destructive thing you did.

That's about as ugly a package as you'd ever want to deliver to yourself.

Repentance is how you turn that would-be ugliness into something beautiful.

Christian repentance consists of two steps: being convicted of your sin (that is, really *knowing* you've sinned), and then repenting of your sin.

Think about it: You want two things out of someone who's done you wrong. First, you want them to feel the depth of their transgression against you, to intellectually and emotionally appreciate how flat-out wrong they were. Second, you want them never again to do to you whatever it is they did. If someone who's sinned against you does those two things—regret what they did and sincerely promise to never do it again—then you are free to once again enter into fellowship with them.

You're free to *forgive* them.

And those are the two things we have to do if we want God to forgive us our sins. It's not enough to only feel sorry about a sin we've committed; we must also determine to never again commit that sin.

Anyone can feel bad. *Doing* something about the fact that you feel bad is where the wheat and the chaff separate.

Regret without resolve is just . . . mawkishness.

"Get behind me, Satan!" means, "I'm turning my back on you, Destructive Tempter! *I'm going the other way!*"

In Hebrew, "repentance" literally means to change one's direction.

He who truly repents is he who executes one truly unmistakable U-turn.

You!

Turn!

One crucial thing about the act of Christian repentance: It has less to do with actually stopping every way in which you sin (since that's impossible, though it is incumbent upon you to *keep trying* to stop sinning, and you surely can and should radically diminish your sinning) than with the fact that it's through repentance—that is, through our fervent desire to quit sinning—that we realize how utterly dependent we are upon God to effect any real change in our lives.

It's only through really trying to purify ourselves—from, in fact, trying as hard as we can to purify ourselves—that we realize what an utterly futile endeavor that is.

Repentance isn't about rules, and oppression, and straitlacing you into behaving like the good little moral Christian soldier you're supposed to be.

Repentance is about stepping into your deepest possible relationship with the highest order of being.

> Repent, then, and turn to God, so that your sins may be wiped out, that times of refreshing may come from the Lord. (Acts 3:19)

> First to those in Damascus, then to those in Jerusalem and in all Judea, and to the Gentiles also, I [Paul] preached that they should repent and turn to God and prove their repentance by their deeds. (Acts 26:20)

> Then Jesus told them this parable: "Suppose one of you has a hundred sheep and loses one of them. Does he not leave the ninety-nine in the open country and go after the lost sheep until he finds it? And when he finds it, he joyfully puts it on his shoulders and goes home. Then he calls his friends and neighbors together and says, 'Rejoice with me; I have found my lost sheep.' I tell you that in the same way there will be more rejoicing in heaven over one sinner who repents than over ninety-nine righteous persons who do not need to repent" (Luke 15:3–7).

"The time has come," he [Jesus] said. "The kingdom of
God is near. Repent and believe the good news!" (Mark
1:15).

Want to know how to begin a life of repentance? Do the next
right thing that's immediately before you. Then do the next right
thing after that. And then the next—and the next, and the next.
That really is one of the best guides for all of us in any circum-
stance, but particularly after we've been sinning and are in need
of repentance. Because you're not really repenting unless you're
moving away from where you were and what you were doing to
a new relationship with God. And you *can* do that because of
what Christ did for you.

What is the "atonement" of Christ?

The Christian doctrine of atonement amounts to this dynamic:
People sin. They always have; in this life, they always will. As we
have seen, sin is part and parcel of human nature.

That people have always sinned and will always sin leaves
in the wake of us all, both individually and cumulatively as a
race, an incomputably vast backload of emotional, psychological, and spiritual detritus. When we sin, we do real if intangible or immeasurable damage to the loving, omnipresent spirit
of God. Through the course of simply being alive (if not by
purposeful, evil intent), we leave the disembodied, numinous
debris of our sins to be dealt with, in whatever degree and by
whatever process, by other people, other orbits of concern,
other generations.

We keep that extra five dollars the cashier unknowingly gave
us; we secretly take that extra half hour for lunch; we go ahead
and make that joke at someone else's expense . . . and then we
move on. And the spiritual debris our sins produce—that guilt and
resentment and dishonor and shame that, in whatever measure,

it inevitably generates—builds up everywhere behind and around us, and in one way or another drags us all down.

And in our wildest dreams, it all just disappears.

How we long to go through life, unencumbered by the weight of our and others' sins!

That's the dream. That's what we all *really* mean when we talk about paradise, about being free, about getting away from it all. When we talk and think in such terms we have in mind existing, if only for a moment, outside the cycle of sin and its cost.

But we know we can't step outside that cycle. We know we're grounded in it. We know we can't make the world's negativity go away. We all know that we mere mortals could no sooner relieve ourselves of the burden of sin than we could hang a second moon in the sky.

We all know that on our own we are stuck, suffering the effects of what we cause.

And what, finally, *is* the effect of our sin?

The Bible answers this in six words (see Romans 6:23): "The wages [that is, the consequence] of sin is death." And we'd know that, too, even without the Bible telling us. We all know about the "wages" of our collective sins. We understand that ultimately sin leads to the undermining and destruction of everything we hold dear. We know that sin begets pain, evil, and caustic guilt. We know it leads to the degradation of our race, the despair of our children, shame about the past, confusion about the present, hopelessness about the future.

We know that sin drives a wedge between us and everything holy and divine. We know that it separates us from God.

Oh, but that sins' results were off of us! Gone! Forever!

Oh, but that we could really and truly live the dream.

Well, guess what, brothers and sisters? We can! Freeing humankind from the terrible results of sin is the *exact* reason and purpose for which Jesus came into the world.

This dynamic, right here—this *reality* of the atonement—is ground zero for Christianity.

The atonement is that miraculous dynamic by which Jesus willfully allowed himself to be slaughtered—to be, as you've no doubt heard it put before, sacrificed—in atonement for our sins. He collected onto himself *all* the results of *all* of the sinning that *all* of us would *ever* do—and then he obliterated it into nothingness.

Jesus Christ died for our sins. With his body he paid the final price for everything bad any of us would ever do. That's where the phrase comes from about believers being "washed clean by the blood of Christ." (See the ending of our response to the Question, "Why is it important that Christians confess their sins?" on page 115.) Sure, that expression is almost repellingly visceral—but it'd have to be in order to capture the terrible, awesome truth upon which our faith in Jesus is founded. Understanding and believing that Jesus died for our sins is what Christianity *is*.

Christ traded himself—God, in human form, *sacrificed* himself—in exchange for the final and irretrievable absolution of the effects of all the human sin that ever has been or will be committed.

See, now *that's* a faith to cling to. That's a god who can do a person some very real, very immediate good. For one (and talk about your Basic Biggie), it provides a way for any and all who believe in what Christ did on the cross to avail themselves of what he did there.

The atonement allows Christians to have their sins utterly and completely forgiven.

You know that guilt you feel when through your sinning—your selfishness, your greed, your mean-spiritedness, your negativity—you add to the Sea of Spiritual Sludge that you just *know* is forever swirling around your feet and legs, dragging you down?

Confess your sins to God, and *voila,* that water becomes clean: you're then free to jump and run and have real fun; you're back in the game. (Again, see the Question, "Why is it important that Christians confess their sins?" on page 115.)

The atonement immeasurably helps you in this life by providing the means of relieving yourself of guilt and shame. And it mega-immeasurably helps you in the next life, by assuring you that not only will you *not* perish after you die, you'll spend eternity basking in the glorious light of God's direct, divine presence.

Because Christ, through his infinite love and compassion, gave his life as a ransom to secure for all eternity the absolute atonement for your sins, you, as a believer in him, get to die without the rancid stink of sin on you.

The atonement of Jesus Christ allows you to die as you never lived: perfect.

And it's dying as clean as the Lord himself that upon your death will render you suitable to not only come into his blessed presence, but to spend the rest of eternity there.

Can we get an amen?

Even the Son of Man did not come to be served, but to serve, and to give his life as a ransom for many. (Mark 10:45)

This is love: not that we loved God, but that he loved us and sent his Son as an atoning sacrifice for our sins. (1 John 4:10)

He who did not spare his own Son, but gave him up for us all—how will he not also, along with him, graciously give us all things? (Romans 8:32)

What I [Paul] received I passed on to you as of first importance: that Christ died for our sins according to the Scriptures. (1 Corinthians 15:3)

He is the atoning sacrifice for our sins, and not only for ours but also for the sins of the whole world. (1 John 2:2)

God presented him as a sacrifice of atonement, through faith in his blood. He did this to demonstrate his justice, because in his forbearance he had left the sins committed beforehand unpunished. (Romans 3:25)

This is my blood of the covenant, which is poured out for many for the forgiveness of sins. (Matthew 26:28)

For God so loved the world that he gave his one and only Son, that whoever believes in him shall not perish but have eternal life. (John 3:16)

For God so loved the world that he gave his one and only Son, that whoever believes in him shall not perish but have eternal life. (John 3:16)

For God so loved the world that he gave his one and only Son, that whoever believes in him shall not perish but have eternal life. (John 3:16)

For God so loved the world that he gave his one and only Son, that whoever believes in him shall not perish but have eternal life. (John 3:16)

For God so loved the world that he gave his one and only Son, that whoever believes in him shall not perish but have eternal life. (John 3:16)

(Hey, it can't be said too many times. But we'll stop now. Barely.)

Just one little observation here that can get us all excited about our faith. All the other religions we've come into contact with are about what we could do for God, and could do to get to God. Big difference when God is doing everything possible to get to us, to sacrifice for us, to save us. And it all was made possible by that amazing sequence of events wherein Jesus died, was buried, and rose right up out of that grave.

Why is Christ's resurrection so important to me?

Because without it there's no Christianity. As Paul so famously and bluntly put it, "If Christ has not been raised, our preaching is useless and so is your faith" (1 Corinthians 15:14).

And there it is. Christ's resurrection—his very definite and in-bodily-form return from the dead after being crucified—is how the validity of our faith is *proven.* It stamps everything Christ said and did as real, true, and eternally alive.

You, I, and everyone else want *proof* of things—and especially about anything as important as whether or not Jesus really is who he said he is. He said he is God. He said he had come to atone for our sins. He said that if we believe in him, we will have eternal life.

That's all wonderful and good. But none of us is entirely stupid—and neither was anyone who was around Jesus during the time of his ministry. Just like we do now, they too needed proof that Jesus is God.

Oh, sure, he raised some people from the dead. And yes, he walked on water, and fed multitudes on nearly nothing, and instantly healed people from afflictions that would have doctors today turning in their stethoscopes.

And those *were* mind-bogglingly impressive miracles, and they certainly had much to do with why, by the time Jesus was killed, vast multitudes were officially having no trouble whatsoever believing he was God incarnate.

But then, after all, he *did* get beaten up, dragged through town, and executed like a criminal.

And when someone who might be God gets himself killed in the horrible, drawn-out, humiliating, extremely *common* way Jesus did, it pretty seriously dulls up whatever luster that person has managed to accrue about them.

And say what you will about Christ, but he *was* killed. Thousands saw it. His torture and death didn't happen in a back room somewhere. It was as public as public gets.

And it really did kill him; Jesus really did pass from this world to the next. As John, who witnessed the crucifixion of his beloved friend, wrote:

> Because the Jews did not want the bodies left on the
> crosses during the Sabbath, they asked Pilate to have
> the legs broken and the bodies taken down. The soldiers
> therefore came and broke the legs of the first man who
> had been crucified with Jesus, and then those of the other.
> But when they came to Jesus and found that he was
> already dead, they did not break his legs. Instead, one of
> the soldiers pierced Jesus' side with a spear, bringing a
> sudden flow of blood and water. (John 19:31–34)

And there it is. That's as dead as a person can be.

Then Jesus' body was put into a tomb.

That was Friday. On Sunday (and despite the guards who'd been posted to make sure nothing happened to the body), Jesus' tomb was found empty.

Not too long after that, all kinds of people saw Jesus walking around, hanging out, talking up a storm, cracking jokes, *eating,* for goodness' sake.

He was back, and no two ways about it.

And again: Very public. When Jesus returned from the dead, he didn't appear as a mystical apparition before one or two people in the middle of the night. He didn't show up in anyone's spiritual visions. He strolled around like he'd just been elected mayor of Happyville.

He came back to *life* life, precisely as he'd said all along he would.

The bodily resurrection of Christ is important because the sheer miracle of it—the crazy, unthinkable power of such a thing actually and truly happening—effectively takes away one's choice about whether or not to believe that the man called Jesus was and is God incarnate.

If Christ's resurrection was real, then Christianity is real. It's exactly that simple, that startling, and that glorious.

Happy Easter. Every single day of your blessed life.

What I [Paul] received I passed on to you as of first importance: that Christ died for our sins according to the Scriptures, that he was buried, that he was raised on the third day according to the Scriptures, and that he appeared to Peter, and then to the Twelve. After that, he appeared to more than five hundred of the brothers at the same time. (1 Corinthians 15:3–6)

If Christ has not been raised. . . . we are then found to be false witnesses about God, for we have testified about God that he raised Christ from the dead. (1 Corinthians 15:14–15)

The angel said to the women, "Do not be afraid, for I know that you are looking for Jesus, who was crucified. He is not here; he has risen, just as he said" (Matthew 28:5–6).

After his [Jesus'] suffering, he showed himself to these men and gave many convincing proofs that he was alive. He appeared to them over a period of forty days and spoke about the kingdom of God. (Acts 1:3)

He was delivered over to death for our sins and was raised to life for our justification. (Romans 4:25)

Jesus said to her, "I am the resurrection and the life. He who believes in me will live, even though he dies" (John 11:25).

Where, O death, is your victory? Where, O death, is your sting? (1 Corinthians 15:55)

A lot of us wear crosses to consistently remind ourselves of Christ's suffering and to honor his indescribable sacrifice. But maybe to this we should add wearing little rocks with empty holes in them, to signify the empty tomb.

That Friday there was a very sad death. But that Sunday, oh man, that Resurrection Sunday must have been one amazing day. A day we can all be "proud" of.

Why is pride considered such a primary and dangerous sin?

Well, right off it depends on just what you mean by *pride*. Taking pride in Christ—in being associated with Jesus, in having a relationship with him, in being aligned with his desires for all of humankind—is something in which a person should take pride. That kind of pride is good.

Too bad it's so difficult to make the good kind of pride *remain* the good kind of pride. Sadly, good pride becomes bad pride just as easily as water flows downhill.

Curse that devil!

Curse our egos! (See the Question, "What is 'original sin'?" on page 111.)

Here's what we mean: "I am proud to be a follower of Christ" is a statement rooted in the good, positive kind of pride to which we've just referred, yes? It's a sentiment to which no Christian would think to take exception.

But watch how easily that simple, honorable statement transmogrifies from humbly *pro*-God to arrogantly *anti*-God. In other words, watch how good pride becomes bad:

- "I am proud to be a follower of Christ." (No problem there!)
- "It's good to be a follower of Christ." (No argument there!)
- "If it's good to be a follower of Christ, and I'm a follower of Christ, then I must be good." (Ego alert!)
- "I am good." (*Ding ding ding ding!* And we have ourselves a loser!)

See what happened? See how smoothly, how readily, how almost automatically "*God* is good" gets turned into "*I* am good"?

And of course it only gets uglier from there. "I am good" almost inevitably sets into motion an insidious chain reaction of attitudinal adjustments that is subtle, caustic, and nearly impossible to resist.

And here's how *that* goes:

- "I am good because I believe in Christ."
- "Since believing in Christ is good, people who don't believe in Christ must be bad."
- "People who don't believe in Christ are bad."
- "In the name of Christ, people who are bad must be given the message that they are bad."
- "It's right to be vocally, harshly judgmental toward non-Christians."

So. You get the idea. This progression—and/or the zillions of personal varieties of it—is one of the ways in which the water of life can turn bitter and poisonous.

The wise believer understands that he or she must be vigilant about not attaching their prideful ego to the glorious truths of Christ. All Christians need to consider pride an especially dangerous sin, because of how quickly and insidiously it can insinuate itself into one's heart and attitude. Going from "Christ loves me" to "I'm supremely lovable" is a perilously short trip. (And one with seductively captivating views, too. Look! There's Mount Arentigreat! And the sweeping Plain of My Knowledge! And see how the Magnificent-Me River sparkles!)

Wisdom says to avoid taking that trip at all. "Pride goeth before the fall" is an ancient lesson that for believers should always remain especially fresh.

> Pride goes before destruction, a haughty spirit before a fall. (Proverbs 16:18)

> God opposes the proud but gives grace to the humble. (James 4:6)

> If you think you are standing firm, be careful that you don't fall! (1 Corinthians 10:12)

We find it interesting that a pack of lions is called a pride, because pride will eat you like a pack of lions. If there's one sin to work on, perhaps it's best to start working on the one that, alas, is always with us—pride.

Is it possible for me to stop behaving in sinful ways?

No, it's not. Absolutely it's possible for you to less often *behave* sinfully; as you rely on the indwelling power of Christ to diminish within you the sort of spiritual malaise or discomfort that so often results in sinful behavior. Gaining a great measure of strength over our sinful ways through the abiding ministrations of the Holy Spirit is one of the personal rewards that come from being a devoted follower of Jesus.

But struggle though we might to totally rise above it, for now we're still bound to our human nature; that nature is fallen (see the Question, "What is 'original sin'?" on page 111) and, therefore, inexorably sinful. It's an unavoidable fact of our existence that within any given day (if not within any given *moment*) we're bound to act or think selfishly, greedily, angrily. In spite of ourselves, we will sooner or later be impatient, gossipy, dismissive, arrogant, prideful, deceitful, opportunistic, and on and on and on and on, till death do we part from this life. Behaving and thinking in ways that amount to our purposefully glorifying ourselves rather than God is what, by virtue of our sinful nature, we are entirely prone to do.

Over and over again we prove to ourselves, to God, and to everyone else that, of all things, we're not yet ready to take our place among the saints.

But—hallelujah!—what's also true is that our Savior delivers us from the feeling of hopelessness that necessarily results from our intractably sinful ways. With Jesus Christ helping us and showing us the way to live a holier, more honorable life—the kind of life that builds up rather than tears down God's kingdom here on earth—we *can* loosen from their grip on our lives the very sins that most effectively block us from thoroughly experiencing the fullness of God's love.

Through persistent prayer and diligent attention, we can succeed at eliminating from our behaviors and thoughts the kind of habitual self-destruction and perennial negativity that mark the hopeless sinner. And in response to those sins that we fail to overcome or eradicate completely, we have—thank God!—confession and repentance. (See the Questions, "Why is it important that

Christians confess their sins?" and "Why is repentance so important to me?" on pages 115 and 118.)

Get behind me, Satan! You are a stumbling block to me; you do not have in mind the things of God, but the things of men. (Matthew 16:23)

We know that the law is spiritual; but I am unspiritual, sold as a slave to sin. I do not understand what I do. For what I want to do I do not do, but what I hate I do. And if I do what I do not want to do, I agree that the law is good. As it is, it is no longer I myself who do it, but it is sin living in me. I know that nothing good lives in me, that is, in my sinful nature. For I have the desire to do what is good, but I cannot carry it out. For what I do is not the good I want to do; no, the evil I do not want to do—this I keep on doing. Now if I do what I do not want to do, it is no longer I who do it, but it is sin living in me that does it.

So I find this law at work: When I want to do good, evil is right there with me. For in my inner being I delight in God's law; but I see another law at work in the members of my body, waging war against the law of my mind and making me a prisoner of the law of sin at work within my members. What a wretched man I am! Who will rescue me from this body of death? Thanks be to God—through Jesus Christ our Lord!

So then, I myself in my mind am a slave to God's law, but in the sinful nature a slave to the law of sin. (Romans 7:14–25)

Be strong in the Lord and in his mighty power. Put on the full armor of God so that you can take your stand against the devil's schemes. (Ephesians 6:10–11)

Sinning, as we've seen, is an intractable part of being human. But that doesn't mean we shouldn't diligently seek not to sin. Being sick is also a part of being human, but that doesn't mean we should stop taking care of our health, does it? And just like there are degrees of sickness, so there are degrees of sinning. Less sinning, like being less sick, is *always* better.

Is there any sin that's beyond forgiving?

The bad news is that Jesus has told us there *is* one sin that's absolutely unpardonable. The good news is that it's not possible for that sin to be committed by a Christian.

Here (in Matthew 12:31–32) is where Jesus specifies what Christian tradition has since named "the unpardonable sin":

> I tell you, every sin and blasphemy will be forgiven men, but the blasphemy against the Spirit will not be forgiven. Anyone who speaks a word against the Son of Man will be forgiven, but anyone who speaks against the Holy Spirit will not be forgiven, either in this age or in the age to come.

Do, by the way, read for yourself the whole passage from which this excerpt is taken. It's very exciting! Jesus proclaims the above in anger to a group of condemning religious leaders (Pharisees) who have just seen him instantly cure a man who'd long been blind and mute. And to what supernatural powers do the scandalized Pharisees attribute the manifest, undeniable powers of miraculous healing? To *Satan!* "It is only by Beelzebub, the prince of demons," they say, "that this fellow drives out demons" (Matthew 12:24). You can imagine (even better, you can read!) how Jesus feels when arrogant, self-righteous authority figures claim that his powers derive not from his loving and benevolent Father but from his and his father's mortal enemy: arrogant religious hypocrisy. The excerpt we quoted is just part of what Jesus, burning with a fury you can *feel* radiating off the Bible, tells his would-be judges: "You brood of vipers, how can you who are evil say anything good?" (Matthew 12:34). Jesus filled with joy is, of course, a beautiful thing. But Jesus filled with anger will also very definitely get your attention.

Over the centuries since Christ walked on earth, oceans of ink have been spent by people striving to decipher and understand the full meaning of Matthew 12:31–32. And those lines *are* a tad challenging, insofar as within them Jesus seems to be stating contradictory truths:

(1) Blaspheming against him personally can be forgiven;
(2) Blaspheming against the Holy Spirit cannot be forgiven.

So pundits and theologians scratch their chins and think, "Hmm. But the Father, Son, and Spirit are one. How can it be okay to blaspheme against the Son but not against the Spirit? I feel I shall be moved to write a twenty-six-pound book on this issue." (Okay, they don't *all* say that last part. And aren't you glad for it?)

Luckily, though, you bought *this* book. And what we have to say about The Unpardonable Sin is that Jesus means this:

I understand why people might say negative things about me personally; I have, after all, presented myself here on earth wearing the cloak of mortality. Some or even many are going to resist me, as I've expected and foretold. If a person doesn't at first believe in me, and speaks ill of me, but then later realizes that I am exactly who I say I am—God incarnate—then I will joyfully forgive that person when they ask me to forgive their former blasphemies against me. No problem. But once a person has been filled with knowledge of my divinity—once my

Spirit has come alive within them—and then they turn
against me? That is unforgiveable. Anyone filled with
the Holy Spirit who then rejects the Spirit has created
for themselves a world of hurt from which even I cannot
deliver them. Not that such a person would ask me to
forgive them, of course, since their rejection of me means
my forgiveness has no meaning or merit with them. That
actually makes what I say in Matthew 12:31–32 a bit of a
play on words. I'm very good with words, you know.

At any rate, you see the point: What Jesus is saying is that you
can doubt and even blaspheme against Christ *before* you accept
him as your Savior—but once the Spirit is in you, you'd better
not turn against him.

Our beloved apostle Paul, author of so much of the New
Testament, is an example of a man who once flagrantly did Christ
unthinkable harm: Before he was saved via his famous "Road to
Damascus" conversion experience (which you can read about
in the book of Acts), Paul was a virulent, dedicated persecutor
of Christians, great numbers of whom he worked very hard to
imprison and have murdered. But once, having been "blinded
by the light," Paul accepted into his soul Jesus as his Lord and
Savior, Christ forgave him all his sins. And Paul, of course, lived
the rest of his life in enlightened gratitude for the gift of God's
grace upon him.

But if he had *not* lived the rest of his life as he did—if any
time after being saved Paul had *refuted* Christ's Spirit within
him—well . . . then that would have made the suffering that
Paul did endure as a servant of Christ seem like a picnic in the
park.

So the short answer to "Is there any sin that's beyond forgiving?" is that there's exactly one: Turning against Christ after
you've accepted him. But that's the only such sin. Christ died on
the cross for the forgiveness of all our other sins, even the most

heinous. If anyone who has done *anything* seeks forgiveness for their sin or sins from Jesus Christ—if they truly repent and truly ask God for the forgiveness he has promised all who believe in him—he or she will be absolutely forgiven. Forever. Period.

"I will forgive their wickedness and will remember their sins no more" (Hebrews 8:12).

God exalted him to his own right hand as Prince and Savior that he might give repentance and forgiveness of sins to Israel. (Acts 5:31)

Therefore, my brothers, I want you to know that through Jesus the forgiveness of sins is proclaimed to you. (Acts 13:38)

[Love] is not rude, it is not self-seeking, it is not easily angered, it keeps no record of wrongs. (1 Corinthians 13:5)

Brothers, I [Paul] do not consider myself yet to have taken hold of it. But one thing I do: Forgetting what is behind and straining toward what is ahead, I press on toward the goal to win the prize for which God has called me heavenward in Christ Jesus. (Philippians 3:13–14)

One of the things I like about the life of Paul is that he had an out-of-body experience and in a sense was allowed to view heaven. Then he came back here, and lived and died for Jesus. If there had been a different way to make it to heaven, I don't think that would have been the path he'd have taken. This has always brought me comfort and motivated me to never grieve the Holy Spirit, but to ask for wisdom and guidance from this amazing supernatural source of power within me. When we feel his "tug," we are motivated to clean up our act and get rid of the stuff that makes no sense in our lives anymore.

Will being a Christian help me get rid of my bad habits?

This question offers us as good an opportunity as any to make this ever-salient point: "Being a Christian" won't help you in any way whatsoever. *Christ,* on the other hand, will always help you in all of your struggles to come nearer to him.

If there's one piece of advice you take from this book, make it that being a Christian isn't about "religion" at all: it's about a vibrant, deeply relevant, *intensely personal* relationship with Jesus.

So now that you know this, let us say that one of the primary effects of being in a relationship with the living Lord is that over time it reshapes you into someone who acts and thinks in a more Christlike manner. That's a big part of the whole point of being a Christian: to slowly fade out the *you* in you and replace it with Jesus (who, as it happens, wants you to be the *most*-you you can be). And if you have bad habits that are essentially destructive, those aren't compatible with Christ's living presence within you. As he changes you, he will lift away from you whatever habits you currently have that are compromising the fullness of his relationship to you. (See the Question, "What's the best thing to constantly tell myself in order to always remember my true and proper relationship to God?" on page 39.)

In other words, the *fact* of being a Christian won't automatically rid you of bad habits. But the *process* of being a Christian will diminish your sinning a little bit every day. All you have to do is keep your eyes on God. Give as much of your life over to him as you can. Continue to increase the amount of "you" that you give over to his divine will. Pray for deliverance from any of your troubling behaviors. Mostly, trust that God is working in, with, and on you, to reshape who you are now into someone both he and you would prefer that you be.

Remember: God, even now, is delivering you from your past, present, and future sins.

> Blessed is the man who perseveres under trial, because
> when he has stood the test, he will receive the crown
> of life that God has promised to those who love him.
> (James 1:12)

> If anyone is in Christ, he is a new creation; the old has
> gone, the new has come! (2 Corinthians 5:17)

> No temptation has seized you except what is common to
> man. And God is faithful; he will not let you be tempted
> beyond what you can bear. But when you are tempted, he
> will also provide a way out so that you can stand up under
> it. (1 Corinthians 10:13)

> I can do everything through him who gives me strength.
> (Philippians 4:13)

When God delivers someone, he sends a deliverer. For example, he sent Moses rather than just plop the Israelites from the land of Egypt into the desert. So while Christ will help you with your habits, hang-ups, and addictions, he will also use others to deliver that help. Whatever you're struggling with, be sure you're connecting with others who've been there and moved out of that deep hole that comes not so much from having a problem but from a problem having you. Otherwise, you'll just keep repeating the same old mistakes again and again, while the new guilt and shame piles onto the old guilt and shame.

What can I do about the guilt
I harbor for something I did wrong?

Whenever you feel guilty for something you've done wrong, there are two realms in which that guilt must be addressed in order for you to feel okay again: the heavenly and the earthly. Heavenly-wise, you must address the alienation from Jesus that your transgression engendered within you; you must confess your sin to God and repent of it, humbly beseeching him to forgive you according to his promise. (See the Question, "What is the 'atonement' of Christ?" on page 121.) Earthly-wise, you must do whatever you can to make whatever amends are necessary to as fully as possible bring yourself back into relational harmony with the person or persons you wronged.

Make peace with God, make peace with whomever you hurt—and you're back in business.

We have already taken a look at both confession (see the Question, "Why is it important that Christians confess their sins?" on page 115) and repentance (see the Question, "Why is repentance so important to me?" on page 118). It's these that right your relationship with God. Let us now consider six steps you should be sure to take in order to right yourself with the person or persons whom your sins have hurt.

(1) Take responsibility for whatever you did.

This step seems obvious, but it's all too easy to step around. Too often we immediately get busy dealing with the effects of whatever wrong we did, without first stopping to let fully sink in the cause of those effects. It's so natural to let scatter away from our conscious grasp the core truth of *our* initiative to do wrong, of *our* decisions to promulgate negativity, of *our* eagerness to personally take on a key role in the devil's play.

No good. If you did something wrong, you must take full responsibility for it. While there are always factors surrounding and influencing everything one does, in the end, you must blame only yourself for what your guilt proves was a moral failing. Be with that truth for a while. Let it sink in. As they say in the psychology game, own it. You can't get busy cleaning your house until you've fully assessed what's *in* there.

(2) Apologize to the person you've hurt.

If the person you wronged is still in your life or can be reached, tell them you want to talk about something, get their full attention, and then clearly and explicitly apologize for whatever wrong you did them. This is where you *show* that you've taken responsibility for your actions. And don't modify or in any way compromise the integrity of your apology. None of that weak "I'm sorry if you took offense" business. *Really* apologize, in language that's sincere and unambiguous.

(If the person you wronged is not available for any reason, then apologize *to* them *through* Jesus. Ask Jesus to carry your prayers of regret to them. Trust that this is exactly what he will do.)

(3) Resolve to never again do whatever you did.

Part of the dynamic of repentance is promising yourself and God that you'll never again do whatever triggered your repentance. Ask Jesus for the ongoing strength to permanently change your behavior. But it's also vital that you step up and do your share of the work in this usually formidable challenge. Take pains to apply the full weight of your mental and emotional capabilities toward understanding whatever factors in your life or personality might have contributed to your having acted as you did. You'll need this knowledge of the origin of your transgression not only to clip the thorny weed of your behavior but to also pull it up from its roots.

Reflecting upon and understanding the causes that contributed to your wrongdoing will guide you toward the best means of assuring that you never redo whatever it is you did. Was your errant behavior typical of the way you respond to stress, or an unfortunate result of a truly unique set of circumstances? The former, of course, presents more of a challenge: Ingrained destructive habits—and especially those triggered by emotional stress—are always difficult to break. If the primary cause of your wrongdoing did, in fact, have more to do with *you* than with anything else—if it's usual for you to have reacted to the events in your life at that time by getting drunk, or lashing out physically, or whatever other negative thing you did—then do not hesitate to avail yourself of the professional help you may need in order to free yourself from your patterns. There's no need for you to try to solve a problem of that magnitude on your own. Volunteering to undergo counseling for your habitually troubling behavior is an exemplary way to prove to yourself and to whomever you offended the seriousness with which you take that offense.

If your error was born of your reaction to a situation that was in some new way challenging to you, then go back over that moment and see if you can't find out what exactly about it tripped you up. Something about it did; something happened that made you extremely uncomfortable or even afraid. Isolate that thing.

Fear is what tends to make us lash out, go hostile, lose control. Be honest with yourself about whatever it was that triggered in you the response you now wish you could take back. Understanding what made you afraid or angry will allow you not only to understand for your own good what dynamic got the better of you, it will also allow you to apologize to whomever you offended in a way that will show that person how thoroughly you now understand the nature of your offense.

(4) Make amends.

Do something to prove your remorse and repentance. Make it good in real terms. Balance the scales of justice. It's one thing to have your boss apologize to you for never acknowledging all the great work you do; it's another for her to *show* you how sorry she is by giving you a raise.

You might ask whomever you've wronged what he or she thinks fair restitution for your offense would be. You don't want to act as if you're asking that person to essentially sentence you for your crime, but it can be helpful to learn what they think would be fair. Your wife might say a month of backrubs would help her forgive you; your friend might say a paid outing or a trip with you might do the trick. Just ask. Maybe the person you hurt only wants you to leave them alone; if so, be sure to scrupulously honor that. The point is to let the other person participate in the process by which you and they are brought back into harmony.

Again, if the person you wronged isn't available to you, make a deeply considered guess at what they might estimate to be a fair exchange for what you did—and then be sure to *do* whatever that is.

(5) Pray for the person you wronged.

Do it every day, and do it for as long as it takes for your guilt to be rinsed away by the healing power of the Lord. Ask him to bring to the person all kinds of joy and fulfillment; ask that he answer their prayers and meet all of their needs. Pray for them and those they love to always be happy, healthy, and surrounded by love.

(6) Let Jesus forgive you.

Open yourself to the forgiving grace the Lord is always waiting to bestow upon those who ask him for it. Sit down, close your eyes, focus on the regret you feel, and then imagine Jesus wrapping his strong, warm arms around you. Let him hug you. Let him love you.

Let him forgive you.

Then, in union with him, forgive yourself.

If we confess our sins, he is faithful and just and will forgive us our sins and purify us from all unrighteousness. If we claim we have not sinned, we make him out to be a liar and his word has no place in our lives. (1 John 1:9–10)

Godly sorrow brings repentance that leads to salvation and leaves no regret, but worldly sorrow brings death. See what this godly sorrow has produced in you: what earnestness, what eagerness to clear yourselves, what indignation, what alarm, what longing, what concern, what readiness to see justice done. (2 Corinthians 7:10–11)

Let us leave the elementary teachings about Christ and go on to maturity, not laying again the foundation of repentance from acts that lead to death. (Hebrews 6:1)

If you sin and then take the path laid out above, you may officially welcome yourself to the Christian life. You are living it. And that comes out of knowing what to do when you've done the wrong thing. Just keep doing this, and gradually you will find you have keener and more reliable discernment between right and wrong.

How can I tell if something I'm doing, or thinking about doing, is the right thing to do?

The short answer is: You'll know. You can always tell when you're doing something you shouldn't: when you've gone too far; when you've acted selfishly; when you've hurt or endangered someone; when you've morally transgressed. Because the Lord's Spirit lives in them, Christians are (or should be!) acutely sensitive to anything they do or say that might in any way be injurious to him. Listen carefully to God within you, and he will tell you if something you've done or are thinking about doing is displeasing to him.

That said, never be afraid to ask for guidance or counseling from a mature believer whom you respect. Life can, after all, offer up all kinds of tricky dynamics and confusing situations, and sometimes we can't help but get so wrapped up in it all that we need someone to help untangle us. It's wise to identify those people to whom you know you can turn when such times come upon you. A pastor, a deacon, an older person who's long been walking with Christ and has seen it all . . . such people can prove invaluable when you find yourself reeling from the ways life can set your heart and mind spinning. Cultivate relationships with believers whose judgment you know is sound. We are, after all, known by the company we keep—and such people can of course prove invaluable when you find yourself in need of godly insight and advice. (See the Question, "How do I best understand, or deal with, 'fallen' fellow churchgoers?" on page 107.)

So the two-part answer is: You'll know. And if you don't, ask someone who does.

We know that we have come to know him if we obey his commands. The man who says, "I know him," but does not do what he commands is a liar, and the truth is not in him. But if anyone obeys his word, God's love is truly made complete in him. This is how we know we are in him: Whoever claims to live in him must walk as Jesus did. (1 John 2:3–6)

We ask you, brothers, to respect those who work hard among you, who are over you in the Lord and who admonish you. Hold them in the highest regard in love because of their work. (1 Thessalonians 5:12–13)

If right now you're feeling the "tug" to make a change or two, tug on the coattails of the wise—those who've proven over and over that their advice is in line with God's truth, and who know how to present that truth in loving and constructive (not manipulative or controlling) ways. But even with those tugs, there are still going to be some simple, everyday questions that will continue to pop up in your life, questions that are perhaps too fuzzy for you to answer right away, but that don't seem problematic enough to present to another. Questions such as . . . hmmm, let's see if we can think of one. . . .

What's wrong with dressing sexy?

The proper or appropriate way to dress while out and about can be a very real concern for Christians—especially young female adults, who more than any other segment of our society are pressured to accept as their own the standards of fashion and looks so aggressively and relentlessly target-marketed by a pervasive, corporate-driven media venally obsessed with the exploitation of human sexuality. (Can you tell we're a little passionate about this?)

It's good and natural for a woman to want to be pretty. And part of being pretty—in fact, the very *definition* of being pretty—is having the way you look be appealing to others.

What too easily goes wrong, though, with a young woman wanting to look pretty—as in appealing, as in admirable, as in manifestly worthy of respect—is that these days a young woman is likely to equate the idea of looking pretty with the idea of looking sexy. And as a look (and, alas, too often as an attitude) it's almost impossible anymore for "sexy" not to get immediately translated into "is available for sex." And that's how a lot of young men are going to interpret a woman's "sexy" look—because boys and men, just like girls and women, have been deeply affected by the hyper-sexualizing of our culture.

Because of the degree to which our society is comfortable considering women as little more than sex chattel, no woman in her right mind would want to go out in today's world signaling that, essentially, she's ready for sex. It's just too dangerous out there. As every female sooner or later discovers, dressing "sexy" is only fun for as long as it takes some creepy guy to start insistently insinuating himself between her and the whole *idea* of fun. And it usually takes about as long for that to happen as it does for a woman to smile and flip her hair.

But beyond the physical danger and the Creep Attraction Factor, there's an even better reason for a woman to make sure she dresses attractively rather than "sexy." It's most definitely *not* pleasing to God when, by virtue of her dress or attitude, any woman makes plain that, first and foremost, she prefers to be considered not as someone of spiritual or intellectual substance, but as nothing more substantial than a body.

If you're a young woman—or any age at all, for that matter—don't ever do that to yourself. Don't ever tell the world that you think the most interesting thing about you is your body. That's dehumanizing—and the devil's primary delight lies in dehumanizing people. Don't make his work infinitely easier by volunteering to do to yourself what he's forever itching to do to you.

Make it so that all people (girls: especially men!) either deal with the whole of you or with none of you. Don't allow your spirit—the real you, the eternal you, the Holy Spirit within you—to be in any way separated from the body God blessed you with as a temporary housing for that spirit. Don't let anyone treat you, in other words, as if you *are* primarily a body. It's wrong for anyone to treat you that way, and it's certainly no less wrong for you to do it to yourself.

> Do not conform any longer to the pattern of this world, but be transformed by the renewing of your mind. Then you will be able to test and approve what God's will is—his good, pleasing and perfect will. (Romans 12:2)

> Among you there must not be even a hint of sexual immorality, or of any kind of impurity. (Ephesians 5:3)

GOD *Outside*

CHAPTER FOUR

The Bible

The Bible is the heart and foundation of the Christian life. But it doesn't do any good just sitting on the shelf. You have to open it up so that it can open up your heart.

The Bible is a thick book, containing many different kinds of writing and spanning thousands of years. So let's get busy learning some vital basic information about the book that in a very real way holds all the information in the world.

What exactly is the Bible?

This is one of those questions like "What is a human being?" or "What is art?" that a person could spend thirty years answering.

You know what? Let's do that. Starting right now, let's spend thirty years discussing the Bible.

Get real comfortable in that chair.

Seriously. Disconnect your phone. You won't need it anymore. And of course you'll have to quit your job. So before we get settled in here, why don't you take a moment to make sure you have someone lined up to feed you and pay your bills for pretty much the rest of your life.

All set?

We're kidding. But only sort of. Because the fact of the matter is you'd be very hard pressed to come up with a more productive or rewarding way to spend your life than delving into the Question, "What exactly is the Bible?"

Talk about your answer that's bound to keep on answering.

Okay: In a nutshell (and as you surely know), the Bible is the Christian holy book. You could say the Bible *is* Christianity captured in print and bound between two covers.

God's purpose is to as fully as possible communicate to us two things: his nature (the reality of who he is), and the depth of his love for us. With all that he is and has, God wants us to know that he *is* love, and that he loves us.

There was never a time when God did *not* want everyone to know these two truths. His whole purpose for making humans, his most glorious and complex creation, is so that we all might come to revel in knowing him, and in knowing how much he loves us.

That's who we are; that's who God is; that's the system we're in.

Well, the Bible is the most comprehensive expression possible of the history and means by which God's desire for people to know and love him worked itself out in real time, over a very long time. Perhaps most important, the Bible is also a reliable guide to and ongoing revelation of how God's will continues to work itself out in the heart and mind of everyone who is or ever will be alive—whether or not any given person ever looks for the truth therein.

Remember: The Bible reveals the voice, will, practice, and purpose of God. And God is everywhere, and knows everything.

And he certainly knows you.

And the Bible is what he has given you so that you can know him.

Get on it! Open one up!

There's no time like the present.

Now for some tacks, of the brass variety.

The Bible (from the Greek word *biblos,* meaning "books") is one book consisting of two books: The Old Testament and the New Testament. The Old Testament is about God and the pre-Christian Israelites; the New Testament is about Jesus Christ, God incarnate, born as a Jewish man.

Both Testaments contain a whole bunch of stuff that isn't strictly historical: songs, parables, poems, prayers, laws, testimonies, prophecies, riddles, allegories, biographies, letters, and more. (The Bible *is* one hefty tome, after all. As we might expect for a book that holds and expresses the heart and mind of God.)

The Protestant Bible consists of sixty-six separate "books" of varying lengths: thirty-nine in the Old Testament, twenty-seven in the New.

It's generally accepted that about forty different authors, writing from the time of Moses (around 1450 BC) to not long after the death and resurrection of Jesus (about AD 100), contributed to the biblical text. We Christians believe that every word of the Bible was written under the divine inspiration of the Holy Spirit.

Almost all of the Old Testament was originally written in Hebrew. Most of the New Testament was originally written in Greek.

Rather than following a strictly chronological order, the books of the Bible are grouped in *types*. In order of presentation, the nine types of literature are:

(1) *The Books of Moses and The Law* (Genesis, Exodus, Leviticus, Numbers, and Deuteronomy)

(2) *The History Books* (Joshua, Judges, Ruth, 1 and 2 Samuel, 1 and 2 Kings, 1 and 2 Chronicles, Ezra, Nehemiah, and Esther)

(3) *The Wisdom (or Poetical) Books* (Job, Psalms, Proverbs, Ecclesiastes, and Song of Songs [or Song of Solomon])

(4) *The Prophets* (Isaiah, Jeremiah, Lamentations, Ezekiel, Daniel, Hosea, Joel, Amos, Obadiah, Jonah, Micah, Nahum, Habakkuk, Zephaniah, Haggai, Zechariah, and Malachi).

Then, in the New Testament:

(5) *The Gospels* (Matthew, Mark, Luke, and John)

(6) *The History of the Early Church* (Acts)

(7) *The Letters (Epistles) of Paul* (Romans, 1 and 2 Corinthians, Galatians, Ephesians, Philippians, Colossians, 1 and 2 Thessalonians, 1 and 2 Timothy, Titus, and Philemon)

(8) *Other Letters* (Hebrews, James, 1 and 2 Peter, 1, 2, and 3 John, and Jude)

(9) *The Apocalypse* (Revelation).

You're probably aware that the Bible is the bestselling book of all time. What might surprise you, though, is that the Bible is also the bestselling book of the year, *every year*.

And here you thought John Grisham and Stephen King knew how to write blockbuster page-turners.

> All Scripture is God-breathed and is useful for teaching, rebuking, correcting and training in righteousness, so that the man of God may be thoroughly equipped for every good work. (2 Timothy 3:16–17)

When you carry a Bible, you're not just walking around with a book. You're transporting a whole library of wisdom and wonder. And as for wondering how in the world to find something in God's library, you'll be pleased to know it's not all that hard to figure out.

To what do citations such as "Matthew 1:20–21" refer, exactly?

That particular citation refers to the gospel according to Matthew, chapter one, verses twenty and twenty-one. References to any biblical passage or verse are always written in this form: first comes the name of the book (Mark, Titus, Acts, Numbers, Zechariah, Proverbs, etc.), then a space, then the chapter of that book, then, if needed, a colon and the pertinent verse or verses of that chapter. So "Luke 4:15–30," for instance, means the gospel according to Luke, chapter four, verses fifteen through thirty; "John 1" means the entire first chapter of John's gospel; "2 Samuel 7–12" means the second book of Samuel, chapters seven through twelve; "Job 1:7" means the book of Job, chapter one, verse seven. Perfect for keeping everyone on the same page, so to speak.

The Bible wasn't originally written that way—at that time there weren't even *spaces* between the individual books, and the letters were *all* uppercase!—but between then and now, some quite-bright people decided to notate chapters and verses so that each morsel of truth would have its own address. Any way you dice it, this was a huge favor to us all.

What is the Old Testament?

The Old Testament is to Jews what the Old *and* New Testaments are to Christians: The Bible. The Old Testament is, in fact, known as the Hebrew Bible. Jews (except for "Messianic Jews") do not recognize the New Testament as Holy Scripture, because they do not recognize Jesus as the Messiah, whose arrival they still await.

Written from around 1450 BC to 400 BC, the Old Testament tells the story of God's unfolding covenant with the Hebrew people, whom he chose specially and specifically to reveal himself. (Hence, the Jews are known as "the chosen people.")

Unlike the four divisions of the Old Testament familiar to most Protestants—Law, History, Wisdom, and Prophets—the Jews divide the Old Testament into three sections. They frequently refer to their Hebrew Bible as the *Tanakh* (often written TaNaKh), an acronym formed from the first letters of the Hebrew words for its three divisions: *Torah* (Law, or Instruction), *Nevi'im* (Prophets) and *Ketuvim* (Writings, or Psalms). Of these three subsections, Jews hold most precious the first five books, which they believe to be God's direct words delivered through and written down by Moses. Most Jewish religious law is derived directly from the Torah.

The good news is that unlike the early Hebrews, we're not required to memorize the whole Bible. Whew! But that's how a lot of Israelites and Jews passed it on from generation to generation. And if you've never read much of the Old Testament, well, maybe avoid Leviticus for a while, and start with some of the great stories that are the heritage of your faith.

As a Christian, do I need to care about the Old Testament?

Only if you want to care about something for which Jesus himself was deeply passionate. Jesus cared so much about the Old Testament—to which he often referred, and from which the essence of his teaching is explicitly derived—for the same reasons any person cares so much about his or her personal history. The Old Testament is the story of God before he himself came to us in the person of Jesus. It is the ground from which Jesus arose; his genealogical, social, cultural, and theological roots are inextricably embedded within it.

The Old Testament is largely—in some ways you could even say mainly—about the future coming of the Messiah. Jesus' extraordinary claim—the miracle of his very life—is that he *is* the Messiah everywhere foretold over so many centuries. He knew that he was the fulfillment of the prophecies given by the Jewish prophets.

The Old Testament is the story of which Jesus personally was the climax.

So yes, every Christian should care deeply about the Old Testament, in the same way a person is naturally motivated to know everything possible about the past of someone they love. If you found a box containing a wealth of information about the background of your father—letters he'd written; stories, poems, and songs others had written about him; photographs of places he'd been and people he'd known; works of art he'd created—wouldn't you dive right into those archives and not stop until you'd read and studied them all?

If you love Jesus, then you should be attracted to the Old Testament, just like you would be to that box containing your father's history. In the most real of senses, this *is* a book about your father's history.

As an example of the degree to which the New Testament constantly reaches back to the Old, here are some passages from the opening chapters of the New Testament's gospel according to Matthew. Note how inextricable the life of Jesus is from the God of the Old Testament.

Matthew 1:20–24

An angel of the Lord appeared to him in a dream and said, "Joseph son of David, do not be afraid to take Mary home as your wife, because what is conceived in her is from the Holy Spirit. She will give birth to a son, and you are to give him the name Jesus, because he will save his people from their sins."

All this took place to fulfill what the Lord had said through the prophet [the Old Testament prophet Isaiah, in Isaiah 7:14]: "The virgin will be with child and will give birth to a son, and they will call him Immanuel"—which means, "God with us."

Matthew 2:2–6

When he [King Herod] had called together all the people's chief priests and teachers of the law, he asked them where the Christ was to be born. "In Bethlehem in Judea," they replied, "for this is what the prophet [Micah, in Micah 5:2] has written:

" 'But you, Bethlehem, in the land of Judah, are by no means least among the rulers of Judah; for out of you will come a ruler who will be the shepherd of my people Israel.' "

Matthew 2:13–18

An angel of the Lord appeared to Joseph in a dream. "Get up," he said, "take the child and his mother and escape to Egypt. Stay there until I tell you, for Herod is going to search for the child to kill him." So he got up, took the child and his mother during the night and left for Egypt, where he stayed until the death of Herod. And so was fulfilled what the Lord had said through the prophet [Hosea, in Hosea 11:1]: "Out of Egypt I called my son."

When Herod realized that he had been outwitted by the Magi, he was furious, and he gave orders to kill all the boys in Bethlehem and its vicinity who were two years old and under, in accordance with the time he had learned from the Magi. Then what was said through the prophet Jeremiah was fulfilled:

"A voice is heard in Ramah, weeping and great mourning, Rachel weeping for her children and refusing to be comforted, because they are no more."

These passages, from the first part of the first book of the New Testament, are about as amazing as amazing gets insofar as they illustrate what makes the Bible such a miraculous creation: Though it's sixty-six books written by forty or more people over some fifteen centuries, it is demonstrably *one* book, driven by one purpose, toward one goal, by one Spirit. These passages show that Jesus fulfilled the prophecies foretold by Isaiah, Micah, Hosea, and Jeremiah. And that's *merely a taste* of the astounding revelations about Christ that one can glean from the Old Testament through familiarity with the New.

Yes, you should be interested in the Old Testament.

Yes, yes, yes, yes, yes.

He [Jesus] said to them, "This is what I told you while

I was still with you: Everything must be fulfilled that is written about me in the Law of Moses, the Prophets and the Psalms" (Luke 24:44).

Do not think that I have come to abolish the Law or the Prophets [of the Old Testament]; I have not come to abolish them but to fulfill them. (Matthew 5:17)

One of the greatest pieces of Old Testament counsel reads, "Wise men store up knowledge, but the mouth of a fool invites ruin" (Proverbs 10:14). Ouch! Most of us have lived that truth over and over again. The best way to live it less and less? *Delve into the wisdom of the Old Testament.* There you will find unforgettable characters that prove repeatedly that truth *is* stranger than fiction.

Who are some of the main/most important people in the Old Testament?

Here you go:

God

Created the universe. Quite famous. Is watching you right now. Back in the day, chose to reveal and very much involve himself in the lives of the Israelites. Being people—which is to say, being prideful and stubborn—the Israelites tended to have real mixed feelings about that.

Adam

Name is from a Hebrew word meaning "man." It wasn't his fault he ate the apple: *Eve* made him do it. (See the Question, "What is 'original sin'?" on page 111.) Famous quote: "The woman you put here with me—she gave me some fruit from the tree, and I ate it" (Genesis 3:12).

Eve

Name means "life-giver." It wasn't *her* fault she and Adam apple-noshed: *Satan* made her do it. Famous quote: "The serpent deceived me, and I ate" (Genesis 3:13).

Satan

Guilty! Forever! Needs to be utterly banished—ASAP. The first of his two big Old Testament appearances was in the garden of Eden. (Infamous quote, from Genesis 3:4–5, explaining to Eve why it's perfectly all right for her to eat the fruit God has forbidden her and Adam: "You will not surely die. . . . For God knows that when you eat of it your eyes will be opened, and you will be like God, knowing good and evil." What a slime bag.) The second big Old Testament appearance happened when Skankboy made a bet with God that he could break Job. (In Job 1:7, Satan answered God's question of where he'd come from with, "From roaming through the earth and going back and forth in it." Can't you just *feel* the ooze dripping off that cretin?)

Cain

Adam and Eve's firstborn son. Murdered his younger brother, Abel. Famous quote (from when, in Genesis 4:9, God asks him where Abel is): "Am I my brother's keeper?"

Abel

Seems to have been a nice guy. Certainly deserved a better fate than being lured out into a field and then whacked by his own brother.

Noah

First, while busily constructing his ark, he might have been the subject of much derision and merriment. Later? Not so much. Famous, pretty-much-wraps-it-up quote about him: "And Noah did all that the Lord commanded him" (Genesis 7:5).

Abraham

Patriarch of the Hebrew race. God established his covenant (that is, made his sacred promise) with Abraham's future descendants by saying to him (in Genesis 17:6–8), "I will make you very fruitful; I will make nations of you, and kings will come from you. I will establish my covenant as an everlasting covenant between me and you and your descendants after you for the generations to come, to be your God and the God of your descendants after you. The whole land of Canaan, where you are now an alien, I will give as an everlasting possession to you and your descendants after you; and I will be their God." And that's the beginning of the long process by which the man formerly known as Abram became "Father Abraham." Famous quote is to his beloved son, Isaac, just as he was about to slay him in obedience to God's command. When Isaac asked where their sacrificial lamb was, Abraham's heartbreaking answer was, "God himself will provide the lamb for the burnt offering, my son" (Genesis 22:8).

Sarah

Abraham's wife. One extremely durable trooper. Famous quote (upon hearing God say that she, an old woman, would become pregnant): "After I am worn out and my master is old, will I now have this pleasure?" (Genesis 18:12).

Isaac

The only child of Abraham and Sarah; the second member (along with his father Abraham and his son Jacob) in the triumvirate of Israel's patriarchs. Isaac's descendants became the Jews. Famous quote about him, by God to Abraham: "Your wife Sarah will bear you a son, and you will call him Isaac. I will establish my covenant with him as an everlasting covenant for his descendants after him" (Genesis 17:19).

Ishmael

Son of Abraham and Hagar, one of Sarah's maidservants. (The then-still-barren Sarah *said* Abraham could sleep with Hagar, if that helps.) Ishmael's descendants became the Arabs: "I will make the son of the maidservant into a nation also," God said to Abraham, "because he is your offspring" (Genesis 21:13). That all three trace their ancestral roots directly to Abraham is the reason Judaism, Christianity, and Islam are considered "Abrahamic" religions. Why these closely bonded faiths have historically been unable to get along is a subject for a whole other, *much* longer book.

Rebekah

The "very beautiful" (Genesis 24:16) wife of Isaac. It was through her twelve grandsons—the twelve sons of her son Jacob—that the twelve tribes of Israel were established; she is thus the matriarchal head of all Israel, and a direct ancestor of Jesus Christ.

Esau

Firstborn of Isaac and Rebekah's twin sons. Big, hairy, hunting type. Exchanged his birthright to his (very slightly) younger brother, Jacob, for some soup and bread. Probably not startlingly bright. Famous quote (and no, we're not kidding): "Quick, let me have some of that red stew! I'm famished!" (Genesis 25:30).

Jacob

Second of Isaac and Rebekah's twins. Definitely bright—and, when young, undeniably sneaky. Third patriarch of the Israelites. Father of twelve sons (Reuben, Simeon, Levi, Judah, Zebulun, Issachar, Dan, Gad, Asher, Naphtali, Joseph, and Benjamin) that go on to produce the twelve tribes. Noted for a dream featuring a heavenly ladder, and for actually *wrestling* with God; God changed his name from Jacob to Israel, which means (unsurprisingly) "struggles with God." New name points not only to his wrestling prowess but also to the tumultuous yet-to-come history of the nation of Israel. Famous quote (in response to Esau's, above): "First sell me your birthright" (Genesis 25:31).

Rachel

Jacob's wife. Inspiringly attractive. ("When Jacob saw Rachel . . . he . . . rolled the stone away from the mouth of the well" all by himself! [Genesis 29:10].) Younger sister of Leah, who through the conniving trickery of their father, Laban (not to mention the culture's acceptance of polygamy), was *also* Jacob's wife. (By the way, how'd you like to be the editor who has to turn the Old Testament into children's stories?)

Joseph

Mr. Coat of Many Colors. Eleventh of Jacob's twelve sons. Sold by his brothers into slavery. His beautiful body and handsome face (see Genesis 39:6) end up getting him thrown into prison (thanks to the lustful wife of his powerful master). Unique ability to interpret dreams ends up landing him a job as the second-in-command ruler of Egypt. Famously dramatic quote, to his brothers, who hadn't a clue as to the identity of Pharaoh's Grand Vizier, before whom they'd traveled a long way to beg: "I am your brother Joseph, the one you sold into Egypt!" (Genesis 45:4). Imagine their surprise! (The story of Joseph and his brothers is among the all-time great page-turners.)

Moses

Arguably *the* major Old Testament figure. A Hebrew who (via an extraordinary series of events) was actually raised in Egypt's royal palace. He murdered an Egyptian; encountered God via the famous burning bush; orchestrated the Terrible Ten (plagues); led the Israelites out of slavery into the wilderness of the Sinai Desert; and, with staff held high, parted the Red Sea. It was Moses, on Mount Sinai, who received the Ten Commandments from God. Tradition has it that Moses also wrote the first five books of the Old Testament. (See the Question, "What is the Old Testament?" on page 156.) As much as anything else, it's Moses' palpable humanity—his fears, doubts, insecurities, reactions—that make him such an inspiring, memorable character. In the book of Numbers, in fact, Moses is described as "more humble than anyone else on the face of the earth" (Numbers 12:3). Famous quote, delivered to the Pharaoh: "This is what the Lord, the God of the Hebrews, says: 'Let my people go' " (Exodus 9:1).

Joshua

Moses promised Canaan to the Israelites; as commander of God's army, Joshua delivered it. A phenomenal military leader: six nations and thirty-one kings (not to mention the fortified city of Jericho) fell before him. Spent forty years as apprentice and then right-hand man to Moses. Prior to the Israelites taking it, Moses sent Joshua and eleven other scouts to reconnoiter the Promised

Land. Ten came back saying the situation was hopeless ("We can't attack those people; they are stronger than we are" [Numbers 13:31].) But Joshua and his buddy Caleb? "Do not be afraid of the people of the land," they said, "because we will swallow them up" (Numbers 14:9). And boy did they ever.

Ruth

Left alone in the world by the deaths of her husband and sons, an elderly Jewish woman named Naomi decided to return from the land of Moab to her hometown of Bethlehem. Ruth, her Gentile daughter-in-law, refusing to abandon her, accompanied Naomi all the way back, and then she stayed with her. Though now a stranger in a strange land, Ruth went alone into the fields of the wealthy Boaz to pick the leftover grain and thus keep her and Naomi from starvation. In the course of one of the Bible's sweetest romantic episodes, she ends up marrying Boaz and bearing him Obed, the grandfather of David, from whom Christ is descended. Famous quote (to Naomi): "Where you go I will go, and where you stay I will stay. Your people will be my people and your God my God" (Ruth 1:16).

Samson

Big! Strong like Hercules! Judge of Israel (as in "leader," as in the book of Judges) for twenty years. Once tore apart a lion with his bare hands. A brilliant brute, who killed one thousand Philistines (who at that time ruled Israel) with a donkey's jawbone. Made the severe mistake of falling in love with Delilah, a Philistine woman; Delilah cut his hair (the source of his strength); the Philistines grabbed, shackled, and brought him into their temple to entertain them; he pushed down the temple's supporting pillars, thereby killing himself *and* thousands of Philistines. Famous quote (said, alas, to Delilah): "If my head were shaved, my strength would leave me, and I would become as weak as any other man" (Judges 16:17). Also famously said (to the heavens, as he pushed on the pillars), "Let me die with the Philistines!" (Judges 16:30). Not the subtlest of fellows. But what a hero!

Saul

First king of the state of Israel. Strong military leader. Eventually grew so jealous of the young, handsome, accomplished, athletic, giant-slaying David (a feeling not helped by the women of Israel singing, "Saul has slain his thousands, and David his tens of thousands" [1 Samuel 18:7]) that one day, while David was playing the harp for him, he tried to kill David by hurling spears at him. The most tragic of figures. Died in battle, by suicide. Fairly startling quote, wherein he states the condition David would have to meet in exchange for marrying his daughter Michal: "The king wants no other price for the bride than a hundred Philistine fore-skins" (1 Samuel 18:25). And you thought a decent engagement ring was expensive.

David

Second king of Israel; the most important Old Testament figure besides Moses. United the twelve tribes of Israel into an increasingly influential nation. His unbelievably rich life is recorded at greater length than any other in the Old Testament. Highlights include: killing the scary Philistine giant, Goliath; becoming extremely close friends with Saul's son, Jonathan; living awhile as the Robin Hood of the desert; twice choosing not to kill Saul, even though Saul was still trying to kill him; becoming king; capturing and making Jerusalem the capital of his new empire; creating a harem by taking wives from conquered groups across his kingdom; impregnating the *married* Bathsheba, then effectively ordering her husband's murder; being nearly overthrown by Absalom (famous quote: "O my son Absalom! My son, my son Absalom! If only I had died instead of you!" [2 Samuel 18:33]); and naming as his successor Solomon, his second son with Bathsheba.

As we mentioned, Jesus' lineage traces back directly to David; in the Bible the Lord is often referred to as "son of David." Indeed David, as the great king-priest-prophet, is traditionally understood as a foreshadowing of Christ. He is credited with writing many of the Psalms, and while it's impossible to pick just one famous quote (what with his having written the *messianic psalms* and all), a definite biggie is something he cried as he was lamenting the deaths of Jonathan and Saul: "How the mighty have fallen!" (2 Samuel 1:19).

Solomon

Third king of Israel. Oversaw the nation's greatest period. Famous for being rich (owned, for instance, twelve thousand horses and fourteen hundred chariots: "rich as Solomon" is no hollow epithet), powerful (his kingdom extended from the Euphrates River in the north to Egypt in the south), devout (he built the over-the-top-opulent Holy Temple in Jerusalem), and wise (he wrote the Bible's Song of Songs, Proverbs [most of them], and Ecclesiastes). Solomon's weakness for foreign women and the gods they worshiped, combined with his treasury-draining, tax-sucking extravagance, set the stage for Israel's downfall under the rule of his son Rehoboam.

Elijah

Supremely important ninth-century BC prophet whose name means "My God is Yahweh." His life was too long and complex for pithy summarization—but in the course of his story, Elijah was: evil-god mocker, king accuser, doomsayer, raven-lover, heaven-sent beggar, miraculous food-conjurer, dead raiser, dramatic-contest holder (between competing gods), prophet killer (of those loyal to the false-god Baal), torrential-rain predictor, lonely and depressed wanderer, kings anointer, killer-lightning deliverer, waters parter, and riser into heaven via whirlwind and a chariot with horses of fire. And that's just in the Old Testament! (Specifically, his story is told in the books of Kings.) Still so prominent a figure in New Testament times that some people thought Jesus and/or John the Baptist *was* Elijah. And when Jesus took Peter, James, and John up a mountain to once and for all show them he was God, whom do you think they saw talking with Jesus in the dazzling vision that transpired before them? Moses and Elijah, that's who. Being pretty much God's number one Old Testament prophet, Elijah said many memorable things—one of which is definitely, "If the Lord is God, follow him; but if Baal is God, follow him" (1 Kings 18:21). This is typical of something people either took very seriously at the time Elijah said it, or later wished desperately that they had.

Esther

Orphaned Jewish girl who lived with her exiled people in ancient Persia. So beautiful, charming, and smart that she ended up being chosen as the queen of King Xerxes. Through sheer strength of character, she thwarted the evil plan of Haman, the king's prime minister, to massacre all Jews in the empire. Instead, the evil plotter himself was disgraced, sentenced, and executed. Yay! Famous quote: "How can I bear to see disaster fall on my people? How can I bear to see the destruction of my family?" (Esther 8:6).

Job

Title character for one of world literature's greatest narratives. Became the subject of a wager between Satan and God about human faithfulness to the Creator. Talk about your difficult test! Job's body was covered with painful boils; all his children were killed; his house and fortune were destroyed. Throughout it all, he refused to curse (though he certainly questioned) God. In the end, God showed his appreciation for Job's unwavering loyalty in a very big way. One of Job's many famous quotes: "Man born of woman is of few days and full of trouble. He springs up like a flower and withers away; like a fleeting shadow, he does not endure" (Job 14:1–2).

And there you have but a few of the key players in this magnificently rich story. And these are only *some* of the interesting characters that show up in the *first half* of the Old Testament! There are whole books from which we haven't yet discussed a single character!

After Job, you have the vastly wondrous book of Psalms, followed by the infinite depth (and astounding practicality) of Proverbs and Ecclesiastes. Then Song of Songs, which has been making romantics swoon almost since the invention of holding hands, blushing, and pining. And *then* comes what in a sense is the climax of the Old Testament: the Prophets. Isaiah, Jeremiah, Daniel, Hosea, Joel . . . and *ten more* divine visionaries after them.

The Old Testament, an Absolute Must-Read? It's hard to imagine for even a moment that it could have for so long held so many people's attention if it were anything less.

Why is asking the next natural question— "Who are some of the most important people in the New Testament?"—like asking why it's so much fun to drive an airplane?

Because it's the wrong question. You don't drive an airplane; you fly it. You *can* drive an airplane—we all know what it is to "taxi" down a runway—but you wouldn't use it to, say, drive on the highway. (Though it'd be fun to simultaneously hog the fast *and* slow lanes!) The main thing about an airplane is that you can use it to help you rise way above it all.

Just as asking about driving a plane automatically steers you (so to speak) away from the plane's whole point and purpose, asking about the New Testament's important people steers you away from the all-critical fact that there really is only one: Jesus Christ. Asking about *other* characters is like visiting an aquarium featuring a blue whale swimming around in a tank the size of the Houston Astrodome, then going up to a security guard and asking, "So, what's the main attraction in this place, anyway?" That guard (once he stops laughing) *will* point you to the blue whale.

And Jesus, as you surely know, is the blue whale in the aquarium of the New Testament.

Which isn't to say that Jesus is the New Testament's only person. There are all kinds of people: tax collectors, prostitutes, kings, beggars, disciples, criminals, pedants, obnoxious pedants, *seriously* obnoxious pedants, children, madmen, starving throngs, blind people, crippled people, formerly dead people, people who don't "get" Jesus, people who get Jesus, and people who *really* get Jesus (since Jesus turned them from corpses back into living people). But everyone in the New Testament who *isn't* Jesus is only in the book because of their relationship with him.

Jesus is the maypole around which everyone else dances.

The Old Testament is all about the role that people's struggles and triumphs played in the long journey through history toward the moment when God the Messiah would come to earth. And then, with the New Testament, we *have* that moment!

There he is!

God became man!

Right here on earth!

Just astounding.

The Old Testament is where you follow the trajectory of the just-launched firework as it races its way up into the night sky.

The New Testament is the moment the darkness explodes into dazzling light.

The Old Testament is the sky.

The New Testament is the sun.

And speaking of the sun. You may be wondering how many times it came up and went down between the Old and New Testaments. If so . . . next question.

How much time passed between the Testaments?

Known as the intertestamental period—and often referred to as "the silent years"—the period between the Old and New Testaments is about four centuries. (That window of time, by the way, was *anything* but silent. You know how in modern times the Middle East tends to be a region of considerable dynamism, ferment, and change? Well, the area has *always* been like that. What's fascinating about the political, religious, and social events of "the silent years" in the Holy Land and its surrounding territory is how perfectly they prepared the stage of history for the appearance of Jesus Christ, the king of a newly ordered heaven and earth.)

Four hundred years is a long time to be quiet, but as you know, our timeless God has always had all the time in the world. Now on to some more big words.

What is the Pentateuch?

It's an older name for the Torah (see the Question, "What is the Old Testament?" on page 156). *Pentateuch* comes from the Greek word meaning "five cases," referring to the five boxes or sheaths in which the scrolls of the Torah were originally stored.

I know, I wish they could have just stuck with one name for everything, but that's what happens when a bunch of intellectuals get hold of Scripture. Here's the next thing they did.

What is the Septuagint?

The Bible as we have it today wasn't simply handed to man by God; people had to decide what books did and didn't make it into what's called the *canon* (Official Collection of Writings) of the Bible. Among the most important are the seventy-two scholars who, according to tradition, came together around 250 BC in Alexandria, Egypt (then one of the world's greatest centers of learning), to translate the Pentateuch from its original Hebrew into Greek.

(The reason Ptolemy, the Greek ruler of Egypt, requested this translation was that by then so few Jews throughout the vast Greek empire spoke Hebrew. "The laws of the Jews are worth transcribing," Demetrius, of the renowned Royal Library of Alexandria, is reported to have said to Ptolemy. "But they need to be translated, for in the country of the Jews they use a peculiar alphabet." Ptolemy, presumably, answered, "Cool. Let's translate it.")

The resultant volume—which took at least one hundred years to finish and eventually included the entire Old Testament—is known as the *Septuagint* (from the Latin word for "seventy," for the seventy or so scholars who are said to have launched the work; it's also known as "LXX," the Roman numeral for seventy). The Septuagint is pivotal in the history of Christianity because it quickly became *the* Old Testament for Jews throughout the Greek (and then Roman) Empire. Additionally, it opened up the Bible—and with it, the idea that a Messiah might be in *everyone's* future—to the non-Jewish world.

In the time of Christ, the Septuagint was accepted as the hands-down authoritative translation of the Hebrew Bible; the

New Testament writers relied almost exclusively upon it for their quotations from the Old Testament.

When you hold a Bible in your hand, you're holding the direct result of work done well over two thousand years ago by preeminent Jewish scholars who labored to translate God's language into man's on the island of Pharos, just off the Egyptian coast, in a learning complex that also contained the Lighthouse of Alexandria, one of the Seven Wonders of the ancient world—whose light, as legend has it, was so bright that it could burn enemy ships before they ever reached the shore.

Ever since the Bible's first five books were put together, people (men mainly) have been deciding what is and what is not Holy Scripture. So don't be weirded out that the Bible as we have it now wasn't delivered in a FedEx box from heaven. *Jesus referred to those Scriptures over and over again.* Also, the good news is that everything that's in the Bible is consistent with everything *else* that's in the Bible. Otherwise, a lot of brilliant people—geniuses, literally—whom I know to be Christians, wouldn't be so moved and persuaded by it. But because it's the Word of God, there's no insult to the intelligence of even the smartest person on earth. End of commercial. Next question!

What is the Vulgate?

By the early fourth century AD there was circulating throughout the Christian church, in Europe and North Africa, countless versions of the Bible translated into Latin, by then widely spoken throughout the Roman Empire. Jerome (known to us today as Saint Jerome), was the linguistic genius assigned by Pope Damasus to render one *definitive* Latin Bible. Jerome got busy endeavoring, as he put it, to "correct the mistakes by inaccurate translators and the blundering alterations of confident but ignorant critics, and further, all that has been inserted or changed by copyists more asleep than awake." Seems like the guy for the job, right? Well, he *really* was, and the result was Jerome's masterpiece, known as the *Vulgate* (as in "vulgar," as in popular language, as in what the "common people" speak). The Vulgate was, to say the least, smashingly successful: It proved to be for the West/Rome what the Septuagint had been for the East/Alexandria. Through hundreds of subsequent years, the Vulgate was the Bible universally used throughout European Christendom, and it served as the authoritative base for every Western European vernacular translation that came after it.

Can you believe people used to go to church and listen to the Bible being read in a language they didn't speak or understand—and in some places still do so today? Well, that's because of the reverence placed in this Vulgate. And no matter what language it's in, God's Word is powerful. I'm just glad that now we all have access to even the deepest meanings of the Scriptures in the Good Book.

What is the Apocrypha?

Remember the four hundred years that passed between the Old and New Testaments? (See the Question, "How much time passed between the Testaments?" on page 172.) During that tumultuous period, Jewish writers continued their tradition of writing about God and recording what was happening to their people. By the time Jerome (see the Question, "What is the Vulgate?" on page 174) was translating the Vulgate, many of these intertestamental writings had become attached to or at least associated with the Old Testament, because they were considered instructive and, by some, even inspired. The Greek Septuagint (see the Question, "What is the Septuagint?" on page 173), translated several centuries earlier, contained all the books of the Old Testament canon, in addition to a few of these other writings; in his Vulgate, Jerome included these writings, for which he coined the word *Apocrypha* (Greek for "hidden").

Throughout the centuries various Christian denominations included in their Bible some or all of the apocryphal writings, usually placed between the Testaments. Throughout the Middle Ages the Apocrypha was largely accepted as canonical.

That changed, however, with the Reformation. (See the Question, "What does 'saved by grace' mean?" on page 29.) Perhaps in some measure as a reaction to the Catholic Church, Protestants denied canonical status to any writing outside the established Hebrew canon. In contrast, holding it sacrosanct, the Catholic Church dogmatically affirmed that the entire Vulgate was fully canonical.

Today the apocryphal books are still considered canonical by the Roman Catholic and Greek Orthodox churches, and appear in their Bibles. Protestants maintain that the Apocrypha, while edifying and worthy of study, are not inspired by the Holy Spirit. The Jews never accepted the apocryphal works as part of the Hebrew canon.

The apocryphal books are interesting, and somewhere down the road you might want to study them, or at least give them a read. But as a new Christian, you have enough on your plate with the Bible's sixty-six books. One of the best to start with is the gospel of John, which is a powerful description of who Jesus Christ is and what he has done for us all. Speaking of Jesus Christ . . .

Is "Jesus Christ" a first and last name, like "Bob Jones" or "Chester Finklehockendocken"?

No (and it's *especially* not like "Chester Finklehockendocken"). *Jesus,* which means "God will save," has long been a fairly common name; it comes from the Hebrew *Joshua,* which in Greek becomes *Iesous,* in Latin *Iesus,* and in English *Jesus.* What in Christ's case gives it special oomph is that God (through an angel) told Joseph to give his son that name (see Matthew 1). So it's safe to say that before Jesus was born, Joseph and Mary didn't spend a lot of time poring through *Bethlehem's Big Book of Baby Names.*

The "Christ" part came later—and that isn't a proper name at all. It's a title, an honorific deriving from the Greek word *Christos,* which is the equivalent of the Hebrew term *Mashiah,* which means "anointed." The ancient Hebrews had always been prepared to call their deliverer "The Anointed One," and so—especially after the Resurrection, which definitively sealed the deal, as it were—it was only natural for those Jews who believed that Jesus was/is the long-awaited Messiah to refer to him as Jesus the Christ, or Jesus Christ. And we of course still do likewise.

Remember the movie *Ben Hur?* The full title of Lew Wallace's book was *Ben Hur: A Tale of the Christ.* Just thought you might like to know that.

What are the Gospels?

The Gospels are the first four books of the New Testament, being those of Matthew, Mark, Luke, and John. The titles of these books are often, and more formally, referred to as "the gospel according to" [one of the four], but usually—as in "Let's open our Bibles to Mark," or "Last night I read some of Luke"— they're simply called by the names of their authors. While all four Gospels tell the story of the life, ministry, death, and resurrection of Jesus Christ, each is marked by the individual perspective and sensibilities of its author.

It's very exciting, as though Jesus is standing in the middle of four full-length mirrors, each reflecting him from a different angle, and all reflecting the others. It's an exceedingly *human* way of getting a full picture of . . . well, of God as a human.

And this, of course, is exactly what makes the Gospels so transfixing: They're about *God* walking around, right here on this earth, on the same sort of legs we all walk around on, breathing the same air we all breathe, living this same reality we all share. In the realest possible terms, the Gospels tell the story of God walking, eating, sleeping, teaching, praying, crying, suffering, dying, and freaking everybody out by *returning* from the dead, thereby proving to anyone who still doubted that he was in fact exactly who he claimed to be.

Life can seem pretty boring, right? It's easy to get into a rut, to know you've seen what you're seeing and done what you're doing a million times before. A certain pervasive dullness or ennui is just part of our human experience.

Well, the Gospels are *the* answer to that rut-inducing malaise.

How could they not be? The Gospels are where God, humankind, history, your spirit, and your brain all meet in one place, at one time, every time you avail yourself of their words.

The word *gospel* comes from an Old English word for "good news." That's pretty much the biggest understatement in the history of the world.

It's amazing that in the Gospels we can read the words that came out of Jesus' mouth and hear the very stories he told. Wouldn't it be great if every time someone asked you a question, rather than act like a big shot who knows everything and uses big words as proof, you just responded with a gripping and relevant story? Jesus was a phenomenal storyteller.

What's a parable?

It's a brief allegory or story meant to impart a moral lesson; an excellent definition often used is "an earthly story with a heavenly meaning." Jesus is famous for his parables. About one-third (!) of everything Matthew, Mark, and Luke recorded of Jesus' words is in parable form. Depending upon how you define them ("Was that really a *parable,* or just a simile?" is typical of something the Categorizing Type might ask), anywhere from thirty to sixty of Christ's parables are preserved for us in the Gospels.

If you've ever read any of his stories, you know they're not always easy to understand. They're not just basic tales, where you get a neat little vignette with two animals, an episode, and then a sentence describing what it all means. Jesus' parables are a *lot* denser than that.

A library's worth of books has been written with the intent of getting to the parables' *real* meaning. And such books will always be written, because the parables are fascinating complexities that, miraculously enough, manage to be at once mysteriously unfathomable *and* clear as a bell. It's like they're written in some magical language that gets automatically transferred to the heart rather than to the brain.

Let's look at one of the most famous—the parable of the sower—as told in Luke 8:4–15.

While a large crowd was gathering and people were coming to Jesus from town after town, he told this parable: "A farmer went out to sow his seed. As he was scattering the seed, some fell along the path; it was trampled on, and the birds of the air ate it up. Some fell on rock, and when it came up, the plants withered because they had no moisture. Other seed fell among thorns, which grew up with it and choked the plants. Still other seed fell on good soil. It came up and yielded a crop, a hundred times more than was sown."

When he said this, he called out, "He who has ears to hear, let him hear."

His disciples asked him what this parable meant. He said, "The knowledge of the secrets of the kingdom of God has been given to you, but to others I speak in parables, so that, 'though seeing, they may not see; though hearing, they may not understand.'

"This is the meaning of the parable: The seed is the word of God. Those along the path are the ones who hear, and then the devil comes and takes away the word from their hearts, so that they may not believe and be saved. Those on the rock are the ones who receive the word with joy when they hear it, but they have no root. They believe for a while, but in the time of testing they fall away. The seed that fell among thorns stands for those who hear, but as they go on their way they are choked by life's worries, riches and pleasures, and they do not mature. But the seed on good soil stands for those with a noble and good heart, who hear the word, retain it, and by persevering produce a crop."

This is one of the clearest, most easily understood parables in the Gospels—a fact definitely helped along by Jesus actually explaining what he meant by it. But note that the only reason for his explanation is that his own disciples had to ask him what he was intending to say through it.

And see how he answered their question? He told his perplexed followers that he speaks in parables to those who, unlike them, do not have knowledge of God's kingdom, so that "though seeing, they may not see; though hearing, they may not understand."

Which we're sure cleared *that* right up for everybody.

We'll leave it to you to discern why Jesus chose to answer with this quote from the prophet Isaiah—just as we must leave it for you to, in time, plumb the depths of as many of these amazing stories as you possibly can. For now, we only use the parable (hey! we're using a parable as a parable!) to make this point: When Jesus talks, it's clear that his business is not about spoon-feeding people his message. He's not *accommodating* anyone.

This isn't Aesop. This isn't a fortune cookie. This isn't adages stitched into a pillow. This isn't the lessons you're supposed to learn from a fairytale, or from Mr. Rogers, or even from your pastor.

This is *God* talking.

> Finally the temple guards went back to the chief priests
> and Pharisees, who asked them, "Why didn't you bring
> him in?"
> "No one ever spoke the way this man does," the
> guards declared. (John 7:45–46)

I love that declaration. And I can't *wait* to hear Jesus speak in person. I imagine he still has some great stories left. Surely they're not all in the Bible. There must be infinitely more!

Why are there so many different kinds of Bibles?

Shopping for a Bible nowadays can feel like searching through a field of clover for that special four-leafer: the possibilities seem endless, they all look about the same, and twenty minutes into the hunt you can barely see anymore. If you go to Christianbook. com (basically Amazon.com for Christians) and hit "Bibles," three *thousand* products come up. Some of the categories into which those Bibles are divided are Bride's, Children's, Chronological,

Compact and Pocket, Devotional, Family, Gift and Award, Interlinear, Life Application, Multicultural, One Year, Parallel, Pentecostal, Pew, Reference, Student, Study, Teens, and Topical.

Below *that* way of dividing available Bibles, you'll find listed
"Versions." These include: *Amplified, Ancient Manuscripts,
Authorized Standard Version* (ASV), *Contemporary English
Version* (CEV), *English Standard Version* (ESV), *God's Word
Translation* (GWT), *Good News Translation* (GNT), *Holman
Christian Standard Bible* (HCSB), *International Children's Bible*
(ICB), *Jerusalem Bible* (JB), King James Version (KJV), *Living
Bible* (TLB), *Message* (MSG), *New American Bible* (NAB), *New
American Standard Bible* (NASB), "New" *New American Stan-
dard* (1995 NASB update), *New Century Version* (NCV), *New
English Translation* (NET), *New International Readers Version*
(NIrV), *New International Version* (NIV), *New King James Version*
(NKJV), *New Living Translation* (NLT), *New Revised Standard
Version* (NRSV), *Phillips Reina-Valera* (PRV), *Revised English
Bible* (REB), *Revised Standard Version* (RSV), *Today's English
Version* (TEV), *Today's New International Version* (TNIV), and
Version Popular (VP).

Whew! And you thought finding a four-leaf clover was a
challenge. People have been known to *starve* to death in the Bible
section of bookstores.

Well, maybe not starve to death. But that's only because there's
always a Starbucks within five hundred feet.

The reasons for so many different kinds of Bibles boil down
to three: Different purposes, different translations, and different
audiences.

Different purposes

Some Bibles—sometimes called "traditional" Bibles—offer
the text of the Old and New Testaments accompanied by no, or
minimal, footnotes; such Bibles are made for direct and uninter-
rupted reading.

Study Bibles (sometimes called Student or Learning Bibles) offer throughout their text explanatory footnotes, sidebars, maps, diagrams, and informative essays; they're made to help the reader understand as much as possible about what they're reading as they read it. (Like *The Life Recovery Bible* for recovering addicts.)

Reference Bibles offer extensive indexes that allow the reader to locate the verses in which individual words are used or ideas are dealt with.

A parallel Bible will show multiple translations of the same text in columns laid out beside one another.

An interlinear Bible will run above or below the English text of the Bible its original Hebrew or Greek.

The *Amplified* Bible will constantly interrupt the text to give, parenthetically, the different ways in which an individual word might be or has been translated; this gives the reader a fuller— an amplified, don't you know—understanding of what they're reading.

So you see how different Bibles have different core purposes, which in turn determines the particularities of how a Bible's text is presented.

Different translations

Lots of words; lots of ancient words; lots of ancient words in different ancient languages . . . put it all together, and you have the explanation for why there have been more than five hundred English translations of the Bible.

That there have been over five hundred English translations of the Bible is the bad—or rather the interesting—news. The good news is that the top six of those translations currently account for 95 percent of all English-language sales. So practically speaking, when it comes to buying a Bible, your choices have been pretty effectively narrowed down for you.

The thing to know about translating the Bible is that before anyone—any company, person, school, denomination—takes on such a formidable challenge, they must first decide if they're more interested in preserving the *literal* Hebrew and Greek in which the texts were originally written, or if their primary interest is in communicating to the contemporary reader the *thoughts*—the ideas and concepts—originally meant to be expressed by those words.

If their intent is to keep as much as possible the words, grammar, idioms, and sentence structure of the original languages, then they belong to the "formal equivalence" school of Bible translating. If instead of this literal, word-for-word focus, they prefer to take the thought-for-thought route—that is, if they think it's more important to communicate what the original text *means* rather than what it literally *says*—then they belong to the "functional equivalence" school of Bible translating.

Formal, word-for-word translators seek to present the Bible in its majestic literary splendor; they want to bring the reader into the Bible's world. Functional, thought-for-thought translators seek to make the Bible's message come alive for contemporary readers; they want to bring the Bible into the world of the reader.

The King James Version is the classic example of formal equivalence translating. At the other end of the spectrum is *The Message*. Its translator, Eugene H. Peterson, has won the acclaim of millions of readers with the elegant, eminently readable, prose style in which he has rendered Scripture.

For comparison's sake, let's take a look at four different translations of a very simple sentence, the one that opens the parable of the sower, which we looked at above.

First, the word-for-word, very formal equivalence-style of *The King James Version*:

> And when much people were gathered together, and were come to him out of every city, he spake by a parable.

Here's the same phrase from the ultra-popular *New International Version* (NIV) (which belongs to a style sometimes called "dynamic equivalence," meaning it seeks a balance between formal and functional equivalences):

> While a large crowd was gathering and people were coming to Jesus from town after town, he told this parable.

Now the same sentence from *The Good News Bible* (GNB), the 1966 version that revolutionized Bible translation by presenting what was then the ultimate in thought-for-thought rendering:

> People kept coming to Jesus from one town after another; and when a great crowd gathered, Jesus told this parable.

And finally, from *The Message*:

> As they went from town to town, a lot of people joined in and traveled along. He addressed them, using this story.

Now, these show fairly subtle shifts, to be sure. But even with this basic, straight-ahead fragment of text, see how we moved from "And when much people were gathered together," to "While a large crowd was gathering," to "People kept coming," to "A lot of people joined in."

Can't you just *feel* yourself loosening your tie as you go along?

And again, that sentence is about as uncomplicated as it gets. Imagine how important such translational variations might become when you're talking about something more abstract than a gathering crowd.

Point is: Read the introduction of any Bible you're considering, to see whether it's grounded in the formal equivalence or functional equivalence school of translating. That way you can approach the text with a helpful understanding of the philosophical and intellectual context in which it was fashioned—and then at some point be sure to acquire a Bible translated the *other* way, so as to continue providing yourself with an ever-increasing grasp of what is, after all, the greatest book ever written.

Different audiences

This is where the whole "Bible as marketable commodity" factor gets pretty intriguing. Every year Americans spend about half a *billion* dollars buying some twenty-five million Bibles. What's also true is that the average American household already owns four Bibles. It's hard to overstate, then, the role creative marketing plays in the feat of selling twenty-five million books to people who already have at least one copy of that book at home.

See it for yourself on shelf after shelf in any bookstore. Bibles for children. Bibles for singles. Bibles for surfers. Bibles for men, like *Every Man's Bible*. Teen-girl Bibles designed to look like fashion magazines. Teen-boy Bibles designed to look like skateboarding magazines. Bibles for businessmen, businesswomen, moms, dads, boomers, students, seniors, athletes, cops, firemen, nurses . . . name any person you know, and very likely there's a Bible geared specifically toward them. And if there isn't—if there's no "Unemployed Chef's Bible," or "Just Moved from Houston to Orlando Bible," or "Irritable-Bowel Bible"— give it a week. There just might be one by then.

This brings us to another reason there are so many translations currently available. Half a billion dollars a year is a lot of money, right? Well, publishers—and, yes, even Bible publishers—are not entirely immune to the call of the profits a number like that suggests. And as we've said, getting a piece of that Christian book-buying pie depends in some part on designing Bibles meant for target audiences within that market. The problem with doing this, though, is that if a publisher hasn't produced a translation of its own, it has to pay for the right to use whatever *other* translation it uses for its audience-specific Bible.

If you're a publisher, that can make commissioning your own translation (as mind-bogglingly expensive as it is) a singularly attractive proposition. Doing so allows you not only to bring to market your own viable, stand-alone translation but to then also use it as the basis for creating as many different kinds of Bibles and Bible-based products as you can discover or sense a need for.

For some Christian publishers, this simply makes good economic sense.

Whether based on the publisher's or someone else's translation, though, it's important to note that all the different kinds of niche-audience Bibles we've been discussing—*The Left-Handed, Recently Divorced Scuba Diver's Bible* and so on—still contain the full text of the Old and New Testaments. Audience-niche Bibles are, first and foremost, *Bibles.* Where they differ is in the additional, para-biblical content—notes, study aids, graphics, cross-references, etc.—that they present in, around, and throughout the biblical text. *That* material is written by contemporary authors who emphasize or draw out ways in which Scripture speaks to the particular needs and interests of that version's intended audience.

It's easy enough to be cynical about the seemingly infinite number of ways the Bible is packaged so that it can appeal to a seemingly infinite number of demographically specialized segments. But there's nothing wrong with helping a reader understand how God's Word can be understood as speaking to them personally. The Bible is an unimaginably complex, infinitely faceted book. It's *good* for every believer to have whatever tools they can get their hands on to help them mine the awesomely rich, life-altering truths embedded everywhere within it.

The *King James Version* (KJV) was translated in beautiful Shakespearian English, and some believe it was finished on William Shakespeare's forty-sixth birthday. If you go to Psalm 46 in the KJV, and count forty-six words from the beginning, you'll find the word *shake*. Count forty-six words from the end of the psalm, and you come to the word *spear*. You won't find that in any other translation. It's almost like a secretly coded "Happy Birthday, Bill!" from the KJV translators to their favorite writer.

How do I know which Bible is the right one for me?

The simple answer is that the right Bible for you is whatever Bible most of the other Christians in your life right now are reading. You're probably going to a church, right? (And if you're not, please see the Question, "Why is it important for me to go to church?" on page 197.) Well, there it is: the Bible that's certainly best for you is the study version of whatever Bible your pastor teaches and preaches from. That's likely to be the same Bible used in your church's education classes as well as the Bible that people from your church will likely be carrying when they show up to small group or Bible study. A big part of coming to know, understand, and appreciate God's Word is doing so in fellowship with other Christians. Using the same version of the Word they're using is a wonderful way to get, and keep, that ball rolling.

For the record, the translation in most widespread use today is the wonderful *New International Version* (NIV). Other extremely popular Bibles with which most Christians will sooner or later come into contact (and, hopefully, read from) are the *New American Standard Bible* (NASB), the *New Revised Standard*

Version (NRSV), the *King James Version* (KJV), the *New King James Version* (NKJV), the *Holman Christian Standard Bible* (HCSB), and—especially these days—*The Message.*

What's a Bible concordance?

It's a reference book that shows every biblical passage wherein every single *word* in Scripture ("if," "and," and "but" included) makes an appearance. A concordance is an outstanding study tool, if for no other reason than that it can serve to consistently inform and enrich your understanding of the Bible as a whole, unified, miraculously interrelated work.

For instance, say you were to use a KJV-based concordance to look up the word *crown*. What you'd find is that in the entirety of Scripture this word appears some seventy times. And if you actually read each of the passages in which it's used, you'd end up with terrific knowledge about the way in which this one particular word has played a whole *role* in the Bible. From its initial appearance in the first book (at Genesis 49:26, where it says, "The blessings of thy father . . . shall be on the head of Joseph, and on the crown of the head of him that was separate from his brethren") to its final appearance in the last book (Revelation 14:14: "And I looked, and behold a white cloud, and upon the cloud one sat like unto the Son of man, having on his head a golden crown, and in his hand a sharp sickle"), *crown* gets used in ways that are so fascinating, and that are at once literal and figurative, and in ways that so clearly work as foreshadowing, that taken as a whole they very definitely make the case that nobody *but* God could have possibly written a book so frighteningly—so *aesthetically*—perfect as the Bible.

And that's just from looking at a single word. Imagine the breadth and depth of territory a concordance enables you to explore.

What's particularly wonderful about using a concordance is that doing so serves to transform the Bible into what it's supposed to be: *your* book. By reading all the ways in which the word *crown* (or *rock,* or *mountain,* or *cross,* or [insert your choice here]) is used, for instance, you will necessarily end up having all kinds of insights, impressions, and thoughts about the Bible that are very distinctively yours, since they were triggered by your interaction with a unique aspect of the text. How your concordance will guide you to read will resonate with *you,* passages will speak to *you, you'll* make all kinds of personal connections and see all kinds of textual interrelationships that will resonate gloriously within *your* spirit and soul.

A concordance helps you find and appreciate the language in which God, through his Word, speaks to you.

Besides the sort of stand-alone concordance we've described above, many Bibles come with a less exhaustive (but still eminently useful) concordance in the back of the book. When you pick out your first Bible, be sure to get one with this common feature.

What's a topical Bible?

It's a lot like a Bible concordance (see the Question, "What's a Bible concordance?" on page 189), only instead of looking up individual *words*, you look up *topics* addressed by Scripture. So in a topical Bible you might look up *hypocrisy,* and then get (in order of appearance) every passage that in some way deals with hypocrisy. A topical Bible is extremely useful, because oftentimes you want to know what the Bible has to say about an issue, idea, or topic that for whatever reason is just then especially important to you.

Without this guidance, how would you know all the places to look for the information you're seeking? If you're struggling with envy, how could you possibly know where in the Bible to find *everything* it ever says using that word? Easy: you look up *envy* in your topical Bible! (Unless you don't have one. In which case, you'd be envious of those who do. Which would only compound your problem. So it's probably best that you go out and buy a topical Bible right now, and save yourself the trouble later.)

Owning a study Bible with a concordance and having a topical Bible sitting alongside it can really help you open up the depths of God's truth from the beginning of your study or devotional time.

What's a devotional?

A devotional is a book that gives you two things: a Bible passage to read, and a brief commentary on that passage. The idea is that every day (most devotionals are "daily devotionals") you read the passage of Scripture selected by the devotional's author for that particular day, and then read and reflect upon his or her own thoughts on that passage. Most devotionals also include at the end of each reading a prayer, which is intended to encapsulate, solidify, and bring closure to that day's devotional time. Devotionals are excellent spiritual aids, since they provide a daily means for a person to read, learn, reflect, and pray. If there's a better way to spend fifteen or twenty minutes (especially every morning), please let us know what it is.

Our experience is that if we don't devote some time to being with the God of the universe in the morning, we're going to be less devoted to his Son during the day. If you're too busy for this, well, like they say, you're just too busy.

Is reading the Bible important to my spiritual growth?

Yes. Yes. Yes. Yes. Yes. Not no. Yes. Reading the Bible is as important to your spiritual growth as water is to a fish.

Imagine that you wrote the story of your life—that you took *fifteen hundred years* to write a masterful book in which you captured everything you ever are, were, or will be.

Now imagine that a person tells you how much they love you, how much they care about you, how much they admire and are in awe of you, how much they yearn to shape their lives around the truths that have defined yours.

But imagine that same person never or rarely *reading* the book you went to the trouble of writing about yourself.

How would you feel about that person?

Now, would you want God to feel that same way about you?

Remember, God didn't spend countless eons forming the world, directing human history, and writing his story—not to mention allowing himself to be flogged, dragged through the streets, and nailed to a cross to be left for dead—for *his* sake. He didn't write the Bible so he could sit around and admire yet another glorious testament to his infinite, unending perfection.

He wrote the Bible for *you*. So that *you* would hear its message. So that *you* would understand its truth. So that *you* would know that he incarnated himself in human form and sacrificed himself in atonement for your sins.

When the Lord Jesus Christ bodily returned to heaven, he left behind two means by which anyone who believes in him can, as often and as readily as they want, prove to themselves that he was and is as real as real gets. The first is the Holy Spirit in you—yours to call upon whenever you will. The other is the Bible—yours to open and read whenever you will.

Any Christian who tries to grow spiritually without constantly availing himself of the Spirit will fail. Any Christian who tries to grow spiritually without constantly availing herself of the Bible will also fail.

And why would any Christian choose *not* to read the Bible, anyway? What fish shoots out of the water, lands on the ground, and thinks, "Perfect! This is the life for me!"

When he, the Spirit of truth, comes, he will guide you into all truth. (John 16:13)

The word of God is living and active. Sharper than any double-edged sword, it penetrates even to dividing soul and spirit, joints and marrow. (Hebrews 4:12)

Research reveals that those who spend twenty minutes a day in Scripture, at least four days a week, not only know more about the Bible and God, but also have added life benefits such as more happiness, better health, and stronger relationships. So what are you waiting for? This devotional time is the habit you've been seeking.

What's the best way to read the Bible?

The best way to read the Bible is in coordination with the Holy Spirit. For that reason it's a great idea to get into the habit of praying before you open the Bible to begin reading, of asking God to open your mind and heart to the full impact of his words. Doing this before you begin to read is more than a spiritual formality. It's essential to fully appreciating Scripture. Since the Bible was written by God through man, it only makes sense that it's best read by man through God. Some say it's not even possible for a non-Christian to read or comprehend the Bible for any length of time; that invariably a non-Christian who tries on his own to swim through Scripture's sometimes murky, always deep waters will give up, finding the text too dense or abstruse to get through.

There's real truth to this. The Spirit is almost like a decoder who works to make the Bible clear to the believing reader. So before you start, say a little prayer to God. Ask him to join with you as you read.

Read the Bible every day. Do what you can to read it first thing in the morning and last thing before you go to bed. Opening and closing each day by spending quality time with God will improve your life in ways you can't begin to imagine if you've yet to make twice-daily Bible reading part of your life. Trust us on this: Your life will go from black and white to Glorious Technicolor. Pretty soon, you'll be just dazzled. It's *that* dramatic a change. Try it, and see for yourself.

As for what to actually read in the Bible, get a plan. At least one of those shelves in the "Christianity" section of your local bookstore will be stocked with books suggesting daily Bible-reading plans. (Better yet, head to a Christian bookstore, and *marvel* at the resources available to you.) Peruse Read-the-Bible-in-a-Year-type books. See what they have to offer, what kind of reading plan each suggests. Ask your pastor and friends what plan they use.

In the end, pick one. And go, cat, go.

A lot of people get hung up on reading the Bible in a year. If that's you, you might try *The One Year New Testament*. I developed it because I was getting hung up in Leviticus.

Should I join a Bible study group?

If you really want to take your Bible reading seriously, the best thing you can do is join a study group at your church. (Also see the Question, "What's a church 'small group'?" on page 221.) Doing so will not only provide you a solid reading plan, it will pretty much ensure that you actually do the reading, since it's a rare person who's comfortable being the only one at a study group meeting who *didn't* do the week's assignment.

That's not why you'll inevitably have finished the week's reading, though. You'll have done the reading for the same reason people in Bible study groups always do the reading: because life affords few pleasures as rich as sitting around with fellow believers who are openly and honestly discussing their thoughts and feelings about the same passage of Scripture. It's just an astounding thing. People you may or may not care to hang out with in regular life become precious to you in a study group. Exactly why must remain a mystery—but it definitely has something to do with the fact that before God all people studying his Word become, if only for that little while, angels. Bible study groups produce in the air a presence of sublime peace, a palpable *divinity* you really must not fail to experience.

It's almost like concentrated, super-personable *church,* in a (very real) way.

So, yeah, you'll do each week's reading. And you'll find that you, just like everyone else in your group, will fairly *crave* the personal insights, experiences, questions, and revelations your fellow group members will share each week.

You know how in intimate, friendly group settings you tend to want to be the one talking? How fun it is to be the one to whom everyone else is paying attention? This most basic of human characteristics changes in a Bible study group.

There, you'll find nothing beats listening.

Where two or three come together in my name, there am I with them. (Matthew 18:20)

The more you read the Bible, the more you realize that Jesus was a connector, and his twelve disciples were his primary group. He modeled what all of us can follow: connecting in a small group, studying together, and together growing toward

God. You'll be surprised at how much you come to love this. Participating—living life—in a group is far different from sitting in a church. One is *going* to church; the other is *being* the church.

CHAPTER FIVE

The Church

In the last chapter we looked at the Bible, the revealed Word of God. Reading the Bible can affect us in myriad wonderful ways. One thing it's bound to awaken in the heart of any believer is a desire to gather together with likeminded souls to worship and praise God in joyful, celebratory fellowship.

Why is it important for me to go to church?

If you're a believer in Christ, it's only natural that you should want to cultivate relationships with others who share your passion for Jesus. The joy that springs from faith can't help but seek to embrace and engage others. Spending quality time with fellow believers is one of life's most rewarding endeavors. If at *least* once a week you don't regularly get together with other Christians (see the Question, "Should I join a Bible study group?" on page 194, for why it really should be at least twice a week) to celebrate and share in the communal joy that flows from everyone there having a deep, personal, and essentially indescribable relationship with Jesus, then . . . well, then the simple truth is that you are compromising the quality of your life.

The bottom line on church is that it's just plain *fun* to be around people whom you know believe and live out the same righteous, holy truths that mean so much to you.

And church is also, of course, about way more than fun.

Church is fundamentally, and always, about God.

The fullest manifestation of God's nature is the love that his children spontaneously share with one another. And church, more than anywhere else, is where that happens. When you're in church, there are no Sam Joneses, or Mary Smiths, or Barney Binkledoppers. In church, there are only "holy spirits" in bodily form, blessedly basking together in the light that illuminates the life of each and every one of them.

You know why people go to church? Because they know church is as close to heaven as we'll ever get here on earth.

Let us not give up meeting together, as some are in the habit of doing, but let us encourage one another. (Hebrews 10:25)

In church, we worship God, who is in heaven. And we also represent Jesus the Christ, who came to earth.

Why is the church considered the body of Christ?

Because that's exactly what it is; that's *what we are*. The church is the very means by which God expresses his physical presence here on earth. How else? Where else do we see Christ more fully realized, more wholly presented, more passionately worshiped, or more deeply understood? When people want to get as physically close to God as they possibly can, where do they go—where *can* they go—but to church?

And without the people that belong to and support it, a church is nothing more than an empty building. It might as well house a post office or a restaurant.

The church is Christ's body on earth. It's where and how in our world God lives, breathes, moves, and acts. It's how he nurtures his believers, how he reaches out to and provides for those who don't yet know him.

Once you've felt Christ within you come alive, once you've acknowledged and acquiesced to the truth of the reality of God within you, you *do* become a cell in the body of Christ on earth. And going to church—regularly communing with a bunch of *other* living, breathing cells of that same body—is the means by which you discover how the cell *you* are is meant to contribute to the functioning and betterment of that whole body.

One grounding for the church as the body of Christ is in 1 Corinthians 12, where we read:

> Now to each one [of us] the manifestation of the Spirit is given for the common good. . . . All these are the work of one and the same Spirit, and he gives them to each one [of us], just as he determines.
>
> The body is a unit, though it is made up of many parts; and though all its parts are many, they form one body. So it is with Christ. For we were all baptized by one Spirit into one body—whether Jews or Greeks, slave or free—and we were all given the one Spirit to drink.
>
> Now the body is not made up of one part but of many. If the foot should say, "Because I am not a hand, I do not belong to the body," it would not for that reason cease to be part of the body. And if the ear should say, "Because I am not an eye, I do not belong to the body," it would not for that reason cease to be part of the body. If the whole body were an eye, where would the sense of hearing be? If the whole body were an ear, where would the sense of

smell be? But in fact God has arranged the parts in the body, every one of them, just as he wanted them to be. If they were all one part, where would the body be? As it is, there are many parts, but one body. . . .

If one part suffers, every part suffers with it; if one part is honored, every part rejoices with it.

Now you are the body of Christ, and each one of you is a part of it. (vv. 7, 11–20, 26–27)

What a great setup—well, until a foot starts wanting to do what only an ear can do. Or an eye wants to start talking. That's where things really get messed up. But when people come together *using their gifts to serve each other,* it's like something right out of heaven.

How do I find the right church for me?

The same way you'd find the right pair of shoes or the right car: You go shopping. Shoes have to fit just right; you've got to test drive a car to know if you really like it; and you need to try a church out a few times before you can tell whether or not it's just right for you.

Churches are like people: they have distinct and unique personalities. You don't automatically get along with every single person you meet; likewise, you're not automatically going to like every church you visit. And if you visit a church you don't feel comfortable in, that's perfectly fine. It only means you haven't yet found the right church for you.

When John first became a Christian some twelve years ago, he figured all Christians worshiped in just about the same way: they sat in their pews; their pastor made a speech and read from the Bible; they all sang a little; they went home. Insofar as he'd ever given it any thought at all, he had no sense that there was much if any variation on this basic procedure. Accordingly, then, on the first Sunday morning following his newfound desire to attend church, John climbed into his car, started driving, and figured he'd pull into the first church he came across. They were all about the same, weren't they?

As it happened, that morning John first came across a Lutheran church. *Now* John is a huge fan of high-church Lutheran-style worship; back *then,* though, he wasn't sure what to think of it. The service started with a man in a full-length white gown slowly making his way up the sanctuary's center aisle swinging a big metal incense ball at the end of a chain. Behind him was a long and stately procession of somber, long-robed clergymen. Bringing up the rear of this curious parade was a man in a thick, high-necked, gold-brocaded robe holding high above his head an outsized book bound in silver that John guessed was the Bible. At that point, though, he was so confounded by what he was seeing that he wouldn't have been all that surprised to learn the book was an ancient tome imbued with the talismanic powers necessary to appease a Mesopotamian god.

Okay, he'd have been a *little* surprised to learn that. But it's safe to say John was out of his element in church that day. For instance, he had no idea what the whole Communion thing was about. The coming forward, the kneeling at the rail, the holding out your hands as if you were begging for something, the deal where *everybody* drinks from the same gold cup (apparently not as unsanitary as he'd always assumed that would be).

And what was this about the "body and blood of Christ"? (If, by the way, you're wondering the same thing, see under the Question, "What are the sacraments?" on page 228.) Were you supposed to chew the little white wafer right there when they gave it to you and just hope you got it down before the giant goblet arrived, or maybe tuck the wafer under your tongue for a bit, so that you could sip the wine without choking or grossing everyone out with your backwash?

One thing was clear: Everyone else there knew what they were doing. And John, not a *complete* doofus, at least knew enough to follow their lead.

But you better believe that the following Sunday John tried out another church, and then another . . . until, eventually, he found one that, a la Goldilocks, fit him just right. (Today, John is an Episcopalian—which is to say, he now worships in a service almost identical to the Lutheran service that, lo these many years gone by, so freaked him out. John would also like you to know he is now the proud possessor of the knowledge that the chain-swinging incense ball often used in liturgical churches is called a *thurible*. And if you'd like to know what a liturgical church is, see the Question, "What's a liturgical church?" on page 223.)

Before setting out to find a church, you'd be wise to ask yourself the sorts of questions that back then John didn't consider. For instance, do you tend to be more liberal or conservative? Do you think you might be more comfortable with a formal, structured, traditional sort of worship, or with a relaxed, more contemporary style? Do you think you'd feel more at home in a smaller, cozy, more intimate setting, or in a giant gymnasium packed with hundreds or even thousands of people?

In other words, before church-hunting, take some time to consider what sort of person you are and what sort of church you might naturally prefer. Because no matter your individual needs or preferences, chances are outstanding there's a church within a few miles of your home that will meet or exceed them.

Also, don't overlook the power of the Web as a tool to help you in your church search. Most every church maintains a site of some sort on which it presents a wealth of information about itself. There you can get a sense of the church's size, the programs it runs or emphasizes, its core beliefs (usually found under "Mission Statement" or "Statement of Faith"), its history, the missions it supports or sponsors, the activities it offers, background and insight into its staff, and so forth.

Once you've attended two or three services at a church that you think might be right for you, don't be shy inquiring about anything specific you might want to know. Definitely make an appointment to speak with the pastor, who should be glad to give you that time. Make sure you bring a list of questions on which you'd like the pastor to enlighten you. Ask about the church's philosophy, its theology; ask for its stance on whatever contemporary issues you think are important. Whatever seems to you a thing worth knowing is a thing worth asking about.

Pastors are usually proud of their churches, and proud of the work their churches are doing. Rare is the pastor who won't want to share with you whatever it is you'd care to know (and, we hope, rare is the would-be parishioner who sticks around any church whose pastor is not entirely forthcoming). Trust that pastors love those sorts of conversations.

Finally, be prepared to be surprised. John and his wife were still looking for the right spot for them when, one Sunday, for no particular reason, they decided to visit an Episcopal church. Within the first five minutes of that morning's service, John's wife turned to him, with tears in her eyes. John, too, had experienced a great welling in his heart.

And just like that, out of nowhere, they both knew they'd found their church.

The wonderful thing about getting involved with a church is getting to know its people. And while you won't always get to know every person who attends your church, at least all who attend know the same person: the pastor.

How big an impact does its pastor's personality usually have on a church?

A pastor's personality usually has a tremendous impact on what amounts to the personality of his church. In a sense, churches are like companies; as you're no doubt aware if you've spent much time in the workaday world, companies tend to very much reflect the personality and character of whoever's at the top of their food chain. Friendly bosses with open-door policies make for welcoming, interactive offices; self-focused, fear-based bosses foster those same kinds of traits in their offices.

The principal, pertinent difference between companies and churches is that CEOs or presidents are usually appointed by corporate leaders, while pastors are usually hired, or at least Officially Approved, by a board comprised of key members of a congregation. In other words, workplace bosses or supervisors are usually appointed from the top down, whereas pastors are usually placed from the bottom up.

In one sense it amounts to the same thing, though: Usually, by one means or another, pastors and their congregants just naturally end up pretty accurately reflecting one another. That's why it's always a good idea to get to know a church's pastor. Chances are good that if you like the pastor, you'll like the church.

When it comes to pastors, character counts. And pastors with character serve. So a great question for any church member is "Does your pastor have a servant's heart?" (It also helps if the Sunday morning sermons aren't boring.) Also, remember that the pastor is hardly the only person who serves to make a church everything it is.

What's the organizational structure of most churches?

It generally depends on the size of the church. A small country church might comprise nothing but a pastor and his congregants, whereas a huge urban or suburban church might have an organizational chart that looks like something you'd find taking up a full wall of the HR department at Microsoft.

The responsibilities of most staff members (who, again, will or won't be paid staff, depending on the church and its resources) generally fall within five pretty standard Church Job categories: Board, Ministerial, Program, Administration, and Facilities. Let's take a quick look at each.

Board

This is usually a group of people who have been attending their church for a long time, care a great deal about their church, have always worked for their church, and are recognized by their fellow parishioners for the quality of their judgment and discernment. A church's board usually hires—and can almost always fire—its senior pastor.

Ministerial Staff

The Senior Pastor defines, articulates, and presents the church's spiritual direction and emphasis. Also does most of the preaching on Sunday mornings. Basically, top dog at a particular divine dwelling house.

The Associate (or Assistant) Pastor has a range of ministerial and/or administrative responsibilities. Think vice president. Many larger churches have more than one associate pastor.

The Deacons/Deaconesses are usually laypersons; sometimes clergy; *always* service-oriented. (The Greek word *diakonos* means "servant, minister, attendant.") These folks tend to be the lifeblood of a church.

The Elders have proven wisdom that's earned them particular respect, authority, and responsibility at their church. (In Titus 1:6–9, we find a great description of an elder's desirable qualities: "An elder must be blameless, the husband of but one wife, a man whose children believe and are not open to the charge of being wild and disobedient. Since an [elder] is entrusted with God's work, he must be blameless—not overbearing, not quick-tempered, not given to drunkenness, not violent, not pursuing dishonest gain. Rather, he must be hospitable, one who loves what is good, is self-controlled, upright, holy, and disciplined. He must hold firmly to the trustworthy message as it has been taught so that he can encourage others by sound doctrine and refute those who oppose it.")

Program Staff

Varies, but typically comprises all or some combination of the following:

The Director of Missions oversees local, national, or international mission work supported or sponsored by the church.

The Director of Adult Education oversees, schedules, and often determines the variety of classes and educational opportunities offered by or through the church.

The Director of Outreach/Evangelism oversees outreach efforts and, essentially, works to get people outside the church inside the church.

The Director of Youth Ministry oversees programs and ministries tailored to the church's teenagers.

The Director of Children's Ministry oversees ministry to the littlest ones!

The Director of Homebound Ministry/Seniors Ministry could be introduced by this promo: "Can't make it to church? Thanks to our blessed volunteers, church can make it to you!"

The Director of Music/Arts oversees construction and major renovations. (But we kid!) What would a worship service be without the planning and direction of music?

Administration

Office manager; finance director/bookkeeper, et al.

Facilities

When you want some *real* work done, who you gonna call (besides the Director of Music and Arts)? Maintenance and care of buildings and grounds are vital to a welcoming church.

And there you have your basic organizational hierarchy for most churches. *Except* for . . . drum roll, please . . . the all-important, ever vital . . .

CHURCH SECRETARY!

People familiar with church life know what people outside it would hardly suspect: It's a *secretary* who's actually in charge of that church. We say this, of course, with slight tongue-in-cheek—but chances are you'd have to do a bit of searching to find a pastor who wouldn't be happy to agree that, for *his* church, this is in fact the case. The secretary most typically knows everything and everybody that has *anything* to do with her church.

Those who for whatever reason deal with numbers of different churches (like salespeople, vendors, government officials, community leaders, etc.) learn one thing very quickly, or eventually wish they had: If you're seeking to become productively involved with any aspect of the life of any given church, then woe be unto you if you fail to make a point of very respectfully beginning with that church's secretary. Try to go around, or over, or for some reason just happen to get on the bad side of the secretary, and it's probable you'll discover that somehow you're unable to ever get hold of anyone at the church; nobody's ever in their office when you call; no one ever seems to receive your messages; no one ever responds to your e-mails, faxes, or letters. If, on the other hand, you give a secretary reason to think well of you, then you'll find that—hey, whaddaya know?—the pastor just happens to have a free hour on Thursday afternoon, or the missions committee you'd like to address is meeting at so-and-so's house a week from Friday, or you've been informed ahead of time that the board meeting for next month has been changed by a week.

In short, most church secretaries see their church family as an extension of their actual blood family. And you know how moms are about their kin.

Just as there are lots of families in any neighborhood, there are lots of Christian "families" throughout our country and world.

Why are there so many Christian denominations?

Although in America today there are some fifteen hundred Protestant denominations (and upwards of thirty thousand worldwide), the real question is why there aren't even *more* Christian denominations. (That said, if you wait ten minutes, there will be. New ones are constantly springing up.)

If you have a sibling—or know anyone who has a sibling, or know anyone at *all*, actually—then you already have a pretty good idea of why there are so many Christian denominations.

People sure like to do things their own way, don't they?

What's important to remember about Protestant denominations is that, in the main, their differences are slight compared to the magnitude of all the beliefs they hold in common. (See the Question, "What's the single most important thing I would have to believe in order to officially qualify as a Christian?" on page 19.)

Those beliefs are wonderfully encapsulated in what are known as the Five Solas. *Sola* is Latin for "alone," or "only": the Solas are the slogans, or sayings, around which the great Reformers of the sixteenth century rallied—and which Protestants still firmly uphold.

Formulated in contradistinction to the teachings of that era's Roman Catholic Church, these are:

Sola fide! (Faith alone!)

Meaning: We can't save ourselves through works; we can't earn our way into heaven. We are saved by faith, and faith only.

We maintain that a man is justified by faith apart from observing the law. (Romans 3:28)

Sola gratia! (Grace alone!)

Meaning: Grace, which is freely bestowed by God, is more than necessary for the salvation of our souls and for our faith in him who saves. Rather, grace is *sufficient* for our salvation and our faith. (See also the Question, "What does 'saved by grace' mean?" on page 29.)

To all who received him, to those who believed in his name, he gave the right to become children of God—children born not of natural descent, nor of human decision or a husband's will, but born of God. (John 1:12–13)

Solus Christus! (Christ alone!)

Meaning: In order to be saved we need no one—no mediator, no priest, no bishop, no *nobody*—but Jesus Christ.

Jesus answered, "I am the way and the truth and the life. No one comes to the Father except through me" (John 14:6).

Sola Scriptura! (Scripture alone!)

Meaning: There is one God, and the Bible is his Word. No other authority is necessary or preferred. In the Bible we have the mind and heart of God, equally accessible to all. (See the Question, "What exactly is the Bible?" on page 151.)

> All Scripture is God-breathed and is useful for teaching, rebuking, correcting and training in righteousness. (2 Timothy 3:16)

Soli Deo Gloria! (The glory of God alone!)

Meaning: Praise, supplicate yourself, turn to, be dependent upon, and be grateful to no one, and (certainly!) to no thing, except to the one God to whom all glory rightfully belongs, and from whom all glory radiates.

> So whether you eat or drink or whatever you do, do it all for the glory of God. (1 Corinthians 10:31)

Those are the major beliefs of Protestant Christians, no matter their denomination.

It is beyond these core convictions that well-meaning, smart, learned, spiritually sophisticated people begin to differ relative to finer or more abstruse points of the faith.

Some Christians believe that anyone can be saved at any time; others believe that only those predestined by God to be saved will be saved.

Some believe that once you are saved there is nothing you can do to render yourself *un*saved; others say it's entirely possible for a person to get themselves kicked right off of Team Saved.

Some hold that a proper baptism always involves an adult believer being totally immersed; others maintain that a few drops of water on an infant is enough.

Some believe women should be in the highest clerical echelons; others argue that women should be mostly seen and not heard.

Some think music enhances worship; others think it detracts.

Some like to dance and shout when worshiping; others prefer to remain contemplatively quiet.

Some sit throughout their services; others have no chairs or pews in their sanctuaries at all.

See? There are all kinds of ways to be a Christian!

People differ. And Americans, of course, having originated from every place in the world, bring to the table of Christianity innumerable histories, inclinations, convictions, and traditions.

When you think denominations, think history.

And history, as you know, is one vast, complex panorama.

Lutheranism began in Germany.

Methodism began in England.

Presbyterianism began in Scotland.

The Reformed churches began in Switzerland.

And, denomination-wise, you too will begin wherever the Holy Spirit first leads you.

Let's take a look at some different aspects of these church varieties.

How many people belong to each of the main Protestant denominations?

It's tricky to answer this with real surety, if for no other reason than that the US Census Bureau's exhaustive decennial census—the ultimate source of information on American demographics—contains virtually no questions about religion. (Being all about the separation of church and state, don't you know.) But through various studies, surveys, and polls, we know that the numbers in America break down to approximately these:

Baptist	35 million
Methodist/Wesleyan	16 million
Lutheran	11 million

Presbyterian	6 million
Pentecostal/Charismatic	5 million
Episcopalian/Anglican	4 million
Churches of Christ	3 million
Congregational/United Church of Christ	2 million
Assemblies of God	1.5 million
Disciples of Christ	.5 million

While these are the main Protestant denominations, some Christian churches don't belong to any denomination at all.

What is a non-denominational church?

It's a Protestant church that seeks to remain independent—that, indeed, forthrightly declares itself independent—of any established, "official" denomination. There is no set of beliefs or practices common to all non-denominational churches (that being pretty much the point), and a non-denominational church does not belong to any larger organization of churches. This, however, certainly doesn't preclude non-denominational churches from being affiliated or in partnership with denominational churches.

Each non-denominational church determines its own specific beliefs, tenets, doctrines, practices, etc.

It's also important to remember that churches come in every size, from one-room chapels to the so-called mega-churches.

What's a mega-church?

A regular church on growth hormones. No, but seriously: A mega-church is . . . well, a very large church. Exactly how large a church needs to be in order to qualify as a mega-church depends on whom you ask, but the standard most often utilized is two thousand regular, weekly worshipers. There are about twelve hundred such churches in the United States, with an average attendance of thirty-five hundred—meaning that every week some four million Americans worship at a mega-church. That's a *lot* of hymns sung and Bibles read (and donuts eaten—but let's not go there).

A mega-church can be of any denomination. About one-third of them are non-denominational, while about 25 percent are Baptist. Being as large as they are, mega-churches tend, no matter their official affiliation, to be functionally and theologically independent. Almost all are evangelical (and about what *that* means, see the Question, "What's an evangelical Christian?" on page 214.) Though more mega-churches exist in California than in any other state, about half are in the South, with another 25 percent in the western US. And half, overall, are located in new suburbs.

If you've never worshiped at a mega-church, give it a try sometime. They're fun (though they take their gospel very seriously indeed). And be ready when the collection plate comes around: The average yearly church income of a mega-church is $6 million.

Here come some questions and answers about the meanings of words or phrases you may have heard come up in conversations with or about Christians.

What's an evangelical Christian?

Deriving from the Greek word for "gospel," or "good news," the word *evangelical* is used so often, by so many, to refer to so much, that at this point trying to pin down the objective, non-contextual meaning of the term is like trying to chase a ball of mercury that's fallen to the ground: instantly, you're all over the place.

That said, we find an eminently serviceable explication to be that offered by the National Association of Evangelicals (NAE), which (according to *www.nae.net*) is "a coordinating agency facilitating Christian unity, public witness, and cooperative ministry among evangelical denominations, congregations, educational institutions, and service agencies in the United States."

Who should know better than these folks what an evangelical is?

The NAE's "Statement of Faith" reads as follows:

We believe the Bible to be the inspired, the only infallible, authoritative Word of God.

We believe that there is one God, eternally existent in three persons: Father, Son and Holy Spirit.

We believe in the deity of our Lord Jesus Christ, in His virgin birth, in His sinless life, in His miracles, in His vicarious and atoning death through His shed blood, in His bodily resurrection, in His ascension to the right hand of the Father, and in His personal return in power and glory.

We believe that for the salvation of lost and sinful people, regeneration by the Holy Spirit is absolutely essential.

We believe in the present ministry of the Holy Spirit by whose indwelling the Christian is enabled to live a godly life.

We believe in the resurrection of both the saved and the lost; they that are saved unto the resurrection of life and they that are lost unto the resurrection of damnation.

We believe in the spiritual unity of believers in our Lord Jesus Christ.

There. That works. Theologically, *that* is what it means to be an evangelical. Practically—functionally, operationally—an evangelical is someone passionate about spreading the gospel to all those in the world who have yet to hear or heed its call to share in the redeeming blood of our Lord Jesus Christ. (See the Question, "What is the 'atonement' of Christ?" on page 121.) And what this means, of course, is that to a very real extent—and certainly in any sort of traditional or classical sense—*every* Christian is an evangelical. For what believer *isn't* naturally compelled to share the Lord's good news?

While such figures—coming from so many different sources, and reflecting the result of so many variables—can only be the rawest sort of estimate, it's pretty safe to say that somewhere between 30 to 35 percent of Americans (or about a hundred million of us) are evangelical Christians.

What's a fundamentalist Christian?

The quick definition: it's a believer who thinks evangelicals are too liberal. Fundamentalists feel that *way* too many Christians, seduced by the allures of contemporary culture, have allowed the core, inviolate truths of the faith to become sullied and woefully compromised by consistently failing to protect them from the pervasive and corrosive effects of our crass, soulless, sex-obsessed, ego-gratifying society.

Historically, "fundamentalism" was simply related to what its adherents believed was nonnegotiable doctrine. If you affirmed (1) Christ's virgin birth, (2) Christ's substitutionary atonement, (3) the Bible's inerrancy, or complete perfection, (4) Christ's bodily resurrection, and (5) Christ's literal second coming and the veracity of his miracles, then you were a "fundamentalist"—as in, you upheld the *fundamentals* of the Christian faith.

Under this original definition, most contemporary Christians would qualify as fundamentalists.

Today, though, "fundamentalism" is almost always connected to additional descriptives. For instance, many follow prohibitions that aren't expressly addressed as such in Scripture (e.g., no alcohol or tobacco, no dancing or movies, no gambling or playing cards, etc.), many maintain a unilateral political conservativism, and many hold fast the belief that the only true and valid translation of the Bible into English is the King James Version.

Fundamentalists also usually believe in "six-day creationism"—the insistence that the earth was created by God in six literal twenty-four-hour days. (As such, many fundamentalists hold that the earth is somewhere between six thousand and ten thousand years old—as opposed to the current evolutionist position that the earth is something more along the lines of four and a half billion years old. Either way, whoever is wrong in that debate is wrong by a *lot*.)

Now, how about an explanation of some things not too easy to explain!

What is "speaking in tongues"?

During their time of worship, some Christians have the experience of becoming so filled with the galvanizing energy of the Holy Spirit that while in something like an ecstatic trance they spontaneously burst into a "language" that no living person anywhere would find intelligible—including themselves. Those who speak in tongues believe *God* understands what they are moved to speak; indeed, they believe that, through the power of the Spirit, they are, during their impassioned vocal outpourings, speaking the very language of God.

The phenomenon of speaking in tongues originates with the miracle of Pentecost, which is told in the New Testament's book of Acts. Here's the core of it (2:1–4):

When the day of Pentecost [from the Greek word
for "fifty," designating the fiftieth day after the
Jewish observance of Passover] came, they [many of
Christ's disciples] were all together in one place [being
Jerusalem]. Suddenly a sound like the blowing of a
violent wind came from heaven and filled the whole
house where they were sitting. They saw what seemed
to be tongues of fire that separated and came to rest on
each of them. *All of them were filled with the Holy Spirit
and began to speak in other tongues as the Spirit enabled
them.* (emphasis ours)

And there you have it: The reason that to this day some Christians still "speak in other tongues" is that when they do so they're
living the reality of the time when the Spirit of God fully descended
upon the church. That that blessed, cherished event is called Pentecost makes it unsurprising that more often than not those Christians who periodically speak in tongues belong to the Pentecostal
denomination or to the Assemblies of God churches.

What is "the laying on of hands"?

It's when one person lays their hands on another person.
Next!
Seriously, did you ever think this book would be this funny?
On second thought, don't answer that.
In general, "laying on of hands" refers to the natural act we
find throughout the Bible, wherein one person, usually possessing
moral and/or legal authority, lays their hands upon or touches
another, and thereby bestows upon or transfers to that person special blessings, spiritual power, healing, protection, or guidance.
The phrase has particular significance to Christians as it
relates to two kinds of interaction: healing, and/or bestowing
the Holy Spirit.

When the sun was setting, the people brought to Jesus all who had various kinds of sickness, and laying his hands on each one, he healed them. (Luke 4:40)

On a Sabbath Jesus was teaching in one of the synagogues, and a woman was there who had been crippled by a spirit for eighteen years. She was bent over and could not straighten up at all. When Jesus saw her, he called her forward and said to her, "Woman, you are set free from your infirmity." Then he put his hands on her, and immediately she straightened up and praised God. (Luke 13:10–13)

His father was sick in bed, suffering from fever and dysentery. Paul went in to see him and, after prayer, placed his hands on him and healed him. (Acts 28:8)

When the apostles in Jerusalem heard that Samaria had accepted the word of God, they sent Peter and John to them. When they arrived, they prayed for them that they might receive the Holy Spirit, because the Holy Spirit had not yet come upon any of them; they had simply been baptized into the name of the Lord Jesus. Then Peter and John placed their hands on them, and they received the Holy Spirit. (Acts 8:14–17)

Paul said, "John's baptism was a baptism of repentance. He told the people to believe in the one coming after him, that is, in Jesus." On hearing this, they were baptized into the name of the Lord Jesus. When Paul placed his hands on them, the Holy Spirit came on them, and they spoke in tongues and prophesied. (Acts 19:4–6)

What is baptism?

It's an outward act that symbolizes the inward phenomenon of accepting Jesus Christ as one's own Lord and Savior. Baptism comes up in the New Testament a lot, and always at a critical time in the lives of those participating in it.

When people are saved—when they've been born again (see the Question, "To what do the words *born again* actually refer?" on page 32)—they are deeply moved to *do* something that shows and captures this glorious reality. Baptism is that thing.

In essence, it's like this: as Christ died and was buried, so the baptized person is submerged under water.

As Christ rose again, so the baptized person rises out of the water.

Under the water is the believer's old, dead life. Out of the water, cleansed by the blood of Christ, is the believer's new, everlasting life!

That is the essence of the divine sacrament of baptism. (See the Question, "What are the sacraments?" on page 228.)

Like anything in the Bible that's plainly foundational to the Christian faith, over the course of two thousand years baptism has been considered and practiced in light of a great variety of understandings and traditions. Today different schools of belief hold different ideas about who should and shouldn't be baptized, and when and how. Some think only adults should be baptized; others believe in infant baptism. Some think you should get baptized as soon as you are saved; others think that being "only" an outward sign means the physical act of baptism can be put off. Some think that, though saved, the believer should wait until he or she has "grown in Christ" before getting baptized. Some churches won't grant membership to a person unless he or she is first baptized in that church.

And then (as mentioned earlier in this chapter, under the Question, "Why are there so many Christian denominations?" on page 208), there's the whole "dunk or sprinkle" debate relative to the physical act of applying the baptismal water.

It's a fair guess that the distinctions we've been discussing mean more to people than they do to God. If you're wondering whether or not *you* should be baptized, first find the church you want to belong to, and then follow whatever course they advise. And no matter when or how you did or do get baptized, rest assured that you're in the best possible company, for Jesus himself began his ministry here on earth by being baptized by (who else?) John the Baptist.

Read it and weep (with joy):

I [John the Baptist] baptize you with water for
repentance. But after me will come one who is more
powerful than I, whose sandals I am not fit to carry.
He will baptize you with the Holy Spirit and with fire.
(Matthew 3:11)

Jesus came from Galilee to the Jordan to be baptized by
John. But John tried to deter him, saying, "I need to be
baptized by you, and do you come to me?"
    Jesus replied, "Let it be so now; it is proper for us to
do this to fulfill all righteousness." Then John consented.
    As soon as Jesus was baptized, he went up out of
the water. At that moment heaven was opened, and he
saw the Spirit of God descending like a dove and lighting on him. And a voice from heaven said, "This is my
Son, whom I love; with him I am well pleased" (Matthew
3:13–17).

You know what has happened throughout Judea,
beginning in Galilee after the baptism that John
preached—how God anointed Jesus of Nazareth with the
Holy Spirit and power, and how he went around doing

good and healing all who were under the power of the devil, because God was with him. (Acts 10:37–38)

This water symbolizes baptism that now saves you also—not the removal of dirt from the body but the pledge of a good conscience toward God. It saves you by the resurrection of Jesus Christ. (1 Peter 3:21)

We were all baptized by one Spirit into one body— whether Jews or Greeks, slave or free—and we were all given the one Spirit to drink. (1 Corinthians 12:13)

And now what are you waiting for? Get up, be baptized and wash your sins away, calling on his name. (Acts 22:16)

What's a church "small group"?

It's a small gathering of people (say, five to twenty in number) who all go to the same church (although outsiders are invited and welcomed), and regularly get together to both study the Bible and enjoy the pleasure of being with others who, like them, believe in Christ. People participate in small groups because doing so allows them to reflect upon and share God's Word in optimal learning circumstances, to encourage others and in turn be encouraged, to form bonds with others, and to pray with others. (The term *small group* is often used interchangeably with *Bible study group*. See the Question, "Should I join a Bible study group?" on page 194.)

Going to small group is in many ways like going to church— only without having to get dressed up! Plus, it's more intimate. Plus you get to talk.

Small groups rock!

A typical small group meeting goes something like this: On

or near the appointed time, everyone shows up at the home of whichever group member is scheduled to host. Greetings are proffered, hugs are exchanged, small talk happens—and eventually (or summarily, if that week's host is more the Let's-Get-to-It type) everyone takes a seat, usually in a circle of some sort, or around a table. Everyone takes out their Bible and opens to the week's designated passage. (They will, of course, have read this passage the previous week. That's right: Small group means *homework,* baby!) Someone will be either that week's study leader or the group's study leader generally—and that person will then either read the passage, or it'll get read in successive parts by members of the group, or whatever.

Point is: That week's passage gets read aloud.

And then the *studying* begins!

Everyone who cares to says whatever they think, know, or wonder about the section of the Bible that's just been read.

It's a wonderful thing to hear from others what a particular passage, story, or even a phrase means to them—and to in turn share what it means to you.

After the study, prayer requests are shared, prayers are said, cookies are eaten, tea or coffee is sipped, hugs are again exchanged, and everyone goes home feeling warmed by the Holy Spirit within them.

A much better way to spend an evening than sitting home watching TV, don't you think?

Where two or three come together in my name, there am I with them. (Matthew 18:20)

Encourage one another and build each other up, just as in fact you are doing. (1 Thessalonians 5:11)

Should I join a small group at my church?

Yes. Definitely. Without question. Yes. Do it. And if you go to a church that doesn't have small groups, start the first one yourself.

What's a liturgical church?

When during the Reformation the Protestant movement sprang from the roots of the Catholic Church (see the Question, "What does 'saved by grace' mean?" on page 29), some branches of the new church, while embracing Protestant beliefs and tenets, nonetheless saw in the ancient forms and structures of Catholic worship much that they believed was worth preserving. They understood that the traditional, ritualized, formal way of worshiping would for many always resonate in a powerful, deeply inspiring way.

Such staples as the procession of vested clergy up the center aisle, the use of incense, the incorporation of religious symbols, the communal recitation of prayers (such as The Lord's Prayer), the congregation's united response to petitions read aloud to God, the observation of the church year (see the Question, "What is a 'church year'?" on page 224), the following of a lectionary (see the Question, on page 227, "What's a lectionary?"), and performance of the sacraments (see the Question, "What are the sacraments?" on page 228), all mark the worship practices typical of a liturgical church.

Liturgy comes from a Greek word meaning "work of the people." And if you've ever been to a service at a liturgical church, then you understand the sense in which its worshipers *do* work. Liturgical churches are very participatory: everyone's always standing up together, or sitting down; everyone prays together aloud,

223

and everyone comes up to the front altar rail together to receive Communion. At many Protestant churches, the congregants mostly sit, watch, and sing together. At liturgical churches, people get (relatively) busy.

The main liturgical denominations in America are Lutheran and Episcopal. (Note the irony that the denomination named after Martin Luther, who is credited for spearheading the radical movement that resulted in churches first opposing and then breaking away from Catholicism, employs worship practices closer to those of the Catholic Church than do Protestant churches of just about any other denomination. Luther may have rejected some Catholic substance, but he still loved Catholic style.)

If you've never been to a Lutheran or Episcopal service, go sometime. Just be sure to wear sweats, because it's like hitting the gym for a workout. We're kidding. But not about attending such a service, where worship can be as beautiful as any you're likely to experience this side of heaven.

What is a "church year"?

The system of hours, days, weeks, months, and years we're all so accustomed to is just one of an infinite number of ways to divide and identify time. A different, ancient way of marking time's passage that's of particular interest to Christians is the church year, also called the Christian calendar or the liturgical year. (You'll also sometimes hear the Christian year referred to as the church's feasts and fasts, or as the seasons of the church.)

From ancient times Christians have used the church year to daily orient themselves relative to the two most significant seasons in the Christian yearly cycle: the period of Christmas (Christ's incarnation!) and the period of Easter (Christ's resurrection!).

Want more *God* in your calendar than you get with only the individual days of Christmas and Easter? Then awaken yourself to the calendar of the church, when virtually every day of the year has a vital and traditionally sacred place in regard to the birth, life, ministry, death, resurrection, and ascension of Christ.

Because the Christian year is rooted in the liturgical observances of ancient Judaism, it shouldn't surprise us that over time different strains of Christianity developed different variations on the church calendar. Commonly, though, the Protestant church year runs as follows.

The Advent/Christmas/Epiphany Cycle

Advent Rather than on January 1, the Christian new year begins on the Sunday that falls nearest November 30. That Sunday through the next three Sundays—in other words, the time encompassing the four Sundays before Christmas—is known as the season of *Advent* (from the Latin for "coming"). During this time the church liturgically, spiritually, and practically prepares for the glory of Christmas Day.

Christmas While Christmas Day is celebrated on December 25, the Christmas *season* lasts the twelve days from December 25 to the Feast of the Epiphany on January 6. (Hence the "Twelve Days of Christmas.")

Epiphany From the Greek for "manifestation"; it's during the season of Epiphany that we focus upon what it *means* to us that God assumed (manifested himself in) human form and died for our sins so that we might have everlasting life. It's also a time when churches tend to focus on their missional work: If Jesus gave his all to save us, then in turn we must strive to see others saved. Epiphany runs from the close of Christmastide (a traditional word for the Christmas season) on January 6 to the beginning of Lent.

Ordinary Time (Part One) This does not mean "boring time

where nothing interesting happens." The term derives from the word *ordinal,* as in "numbered"—and, indeed, the Sundays that fall within Ordinary Time are often designated as such. For example: The Third Sunday After Pentecost, or The Second Sunday Before Lent.

Ordinary Time refers to any period that falls outside the major seasons of the liturgical year. Where within the seasons of Christmas and Easter we focus on *specific* aspects of Christ's life and their meaning to us, during Ordinary Time we think about what Christ means to the *entirety* of our lives. During life's "ordinary times" Christ can, and should, mean as much to us as he does at any other.

The Easter Cycle

Lent A forty-day period (based on the forty days of temptation Jesus faced in the wilderness) of fasting, prayer, self-examination, and repentance in anticipation of the day Christ sacrificed himself in atonement for our sins.

Holy Week Sometimes called Passion Week, because of the awesome and terrible events that unfolded between Palm Sunday (the day Jesus triumphantly rode into Jerusalem on a donkey) and Holy Saturday (the day after Jesus was buried, following his suffering and crucifixion on Good Friday).

Easter Yay! The reason for our joy and hope! Easter is the most important festival of the church year. Every Sunday of the Easter season, which lasts fifty days overall, is a celebration of the glorious resurrection of our Lord and Savior. (See the Question, "Why is Christ's resurrection so important to me?" on page 126.)

Pentecost This day celebrates the occasion of the Holy Spirit first descending upon Christ's disciples. (See the Question, "What is 'speaking in tongues'? " earlier in this chapter.) Pentecost is the last day of the Easter season—meaning it falls on the fiftieth day after Easter. Pentecost Sunday is a traditional day for baptism and for the confirmation of new Christians.

Ordinary Time (Part Two) From the day of Pentecost to the First Sunday of Advent.

And that's the church calendar! Within it, of course, also lie a great many very significant other liturgical days, three of which (for instance) are Ash Wednesday (the first of the forty days of Lent), the Baptism of the Lord (usually celebrated on the first Sunday after the Epiphany), and Trinity Sunday (the first Sunday after Pentecost, when we celebrate the Trinity).

If you're not familiar with the Christian year, consider becoming so. Sharing the seasonal cycle with many other believers to daily put your life in sync with the life of Christ can't help but deepen your appreciation for and understanding of him.

What's a lectionary?

In a liturgical church, every day has significant meaning relative to the life and purpose of Christ. Accordingly, then, every day also has associated with it specific passages of the Bible that believers are encouraged to read and reflect upon. Each prescribed reading usually contains four parts: a passage from the Old Testament, part or all of a psalm, a reading from one of the Epistles, and a reading from one of the Gospels. These scriptural selections, together with the specific way in which they're ordered, make a *lectionary*. (The word also refers to the physical book in which those readings exist, in the way *calendar* can refer to either a system of tracking time or an item you actually pin to your wall.) The vast majority of churches worldwide that employ a lectionary—whether Roman Catholic, Episcopal, Anglican, Lutheran, Presbyterian, Methodist, Baptist, Reformed, etc.—employ the same one, the *Revised Common Lectionary (RCL)*.

The beauty of the *RCL* is that if every day you read the

prescribed texts, in the course of two years you will have read the entire Bible. If every Sunday in church all you do is *listen* to that Sunday's prescribed readings, then in the course of three years you will have heard the entire Bible. And all along, every passage you read or hear will have had special significance for that particular day in the cycle of the Christian calendar.

A lectionary is a thing of beauty, is it not?

What are the sacraments?

You know how sometimes the most basic questions can be the hardest to answer? Well, this is one of those. Back in the fifteenth and sixteenth centuries it was belief and practice regarding the Christian sacraments that had as much to do as anything with the ultimate parting of Protestants from Catholics. *That's* the kind of intellectual, philosophical, and theological history in which the whole issue of the sacraments is steeped. That's a lot of big minds, over a big stretch of time, giving big-level thought to something that's been of central concern to believers for two thousand years.

That said, here's the bottom line: Protestants have two sacraments, and Catholics have seven. Protestantism's are Baptism and the Eucharist (Communion or Lord's Supper); Catholicism's are those two, plus the sacraments of Confirmation, Penance (Confession), Anointing of the Sick, Holy Orders, and Marriage (Matrimony).

The word *sacrament* comes from the Latin *sacramentum,* which means "capital of California" (now seriously, can you believe some people think Protestants aren't funny?). Actually, *sacramentum* means "to make sacred." And that's exactly the idea behind the sacraments: something sacred takes place when they're performed.

We'll here refrain from delving too deeply into the differences between the Catholic and Protestant views on what actually does happen when the rites of a sacrament are given or received. For now, know that a primary difference between the two hinges upon whether or not in the Bible Jesus himself ever modeled and prescribed a given sacrament. If he did not—if in the Bible we never see Jesus administer or receive that sacrament, and never hear him tell his believers to perform or receive that sacrament— then Protestants believe it has no place as a formal rite in his church.

(Remember the section *Sola Scriptura!* [Scripture alone!] under the Question, "Why are there so many Christian denominations?" on page 208? That's largely what this is about: If it's not *explicitly* in the Bible, Protestants say it shouldn't be elevated to sacramental status. We're putting this in black-and-white terms—around the sacraments there are variations in thoughts and practice that run across all Christian churches and denominations—but that's the general idea.)

No one questions that Jesus performed and/or experienced the Eucharist (Communion, or the Lord's Supper) and Baptism—no one doubts that these sacraments were *instituted* by Christ—so Catholics and Protestants have always agreed that each deserves a preeminent place in the church's life and practice. (As a way of emphasizing their non-sacramental theology, Protestants, by the way, sometimes substitute *tradition* or *ordinance* for the word *sacrament*.)

We'll leave it to you to discover elsewhere the reasons why Catholicism goes beyond those two sacraments to the recognition of five others. (Do make a point, though, to avail yourself of the rewards of examining that very thing. Catholic theology is grounded in a love and appreciation of this very decidedly earthy world in which we live, something from which we Protestants, who ever have our eyes on heaven, might sometimes benefit. The passage of the last five hundred years makes it safe to say that at this point, Protestants and Catholics could learn much from one another. What's *certainly* true is that they have much more in common with each other than differences between them.)

So when you hear the word *sacrament,* if it's understood to be meant within a Protestant context, think Baptism and/or Eucharist. If it's meant in a universal or a Catholic sense, think of those two plus the other five.

Here's a quick rundown of all seven sacraments, and what the power of God is believed to accomplish through each.

Baptism symbolizes the cleansing of our sins and our union with Christ and his church, and it symbolizes the death of our old, sinful way of life and our new birth into the glory of his redemptive love for us. (See the Question, "What is baptism?" on page 219.)

The Holy Eucharist (or *Holy Communion*) commemorates Jesus' last meal, shared with his followers the night before he was crucified. By eating the bread and drinking the wine that symbolize his "body and blood," we commune with the living reality of Christ in the deepest way possible.

Confirmation ushers the believer who has come of age into a fuller, more mature relationship with Christ.

Penance (aka *Confession,* or *Reconciliation of a Penitent*) covers with forgiveness the sins of one who has fully confessed them and reconciles him once again with Christ.

Anointing of the Sick uses the blessings of Christ to bring comfort and strength to those struggling with illness.

Holy Orders are used to ordain bishops, priests, and deacons.

Marriage binds man and woman in holy matrimony. (Okay, *that* we're guessing you knew.)

What is "tithing"?

"Tithe" comes from the Greek and Hebrew words for "tenth." When Christians speak of tithes or tithing, they're usually referring to the practice of giving 10 percent of one's income to one's church.

The root of the idea reaches all the way back to Genesis, the first book of the Old Testament, where we find a story of Abram (later Abraham) giving one-tenth of everything he has to the priest-king Melchizedek (see Genesis 14:18–20).

There is no biblical passage anywhere that specifically directs Christians to donate 10 percent of their earnings to their church. Every Christian is absolutely free to follow the Holy Spirit and their conscience to give however much they want, when they want, to whomever they want. Or not.

That said, though, as a rule it's an *exceptionally* good idea for every believer to do what throughout time so many Christians have always done, which is to discipline themselves to give 10 percent of their gross income to their church.

If that sounds like a lot, it is—and that's the point. Many, many Christians, in fact, consider 10 percent of their earnings the minimum they should give. Through their actions, they prove in the realest possible terms that they *do* understand the supremacy of God in their lives; that God *is* always on their mind; that they *do* trust in the Lord to provide; that their eyes *are* as much on the next life as they are on this.

Everyone knows it's better to give than to receive. But knowing a truth and *living* a truth is the difference between looking at a menu and eating a delicious meal. There's just no comparison. One's a whole lot better.

The fascinating thing about regular, automatic, no-questions-asked tithing is that the most compelling reason any person has *not* to do it also happens to be a reasonable motivation *to* do it: pure, unadulterated selfishness.

It really *is* better to give than to receive. That's a fact. Not particularly natural or easy for us to believe, but a fact it is. Giving is *fantastic*. There is nothing else like it to cleanse your soul, to lighten your load, to right you with God and all of his creation.

Giving away what could benefit you so that instead it benefits another is just about the highest order of behavior available to anyone. And because selfless giving is so perfectly reflective of the healthy, holy order of life, it automatically brings to the giver the very best life has to offer: the blessed, divine joy that comes from willfully rising above the selfish, ego-driven, "me first" nastiness that so constantly and subtly undermines the quality of the human experience.

(What people who devotedly tithe also know is that one of its flat-out miracles is that you always get back—sometimes in Actual Money—way more than you give. *Every* Christian who regularly tithes has a story about a particular occasion when, though times were very hard, they nonetheless decided to give to the Lord— and then very soon afterward received a financial windfall they couldn't have begun to anticipate. It's a crude way to say it, but easily the soundest investment strategy in the history of money is: Give to God till it hurts. That's how you end up having all you want. It's . . . bizarre, really. But it sure is true. Again, ask any Christian with a history of tithing behind them.)

You were made to give.

It only *feels* like you were made to get, to take, to hold, to hoard. But that feeling is based on the worst, most caustic lie of all: that you're more important than God.

And about tithing, it's important to note that no one wants or expects you to choose between yourself and God. No one wants you to starve, or move out of your house, or fail to put your children through college or anything like that. God expects you to take care of the business of your life. The money needed to take care of your life is not the money we're discussing. But you know the money that's more than the cost of taking care of your life, the money you essentially waste on frivolous purchases and/or experiences from which you truly gain little or nothing (beyond, oftentimes, weight)? The money that, if you're honest with yourself, you *know* is extra?

That's your tithing money. *That* money you could give to God and his work here on earth.

And that money, interestingly enough, probably comes out to exactly 10 percent of your income. It always seems to work out that way.

Life's funny like that.

Besides, when you give to God, all you're doing is giving wealth back to the source from which all wealth comes. You're only returning to God what was his in the first place.

You know what the bottom line is? Every single person in this world is of two natures: selfish and selfless. Earthly and divine. Animal and "angelic."

And giving is how you instantly promote yourself from selfish, earthly, and animal to selfless, divine, and angelic.

When you give, you become as divine as it's possible to become while living here on earth.

Ten percent, gross, right off the top, every time you get paid— and just like that, your spirit gets to dance around in heaven for a bit.

You want to be a saint, don't you?

Then give. It really is that easy. Because it really is that *hard.* And God knows that.

If there's one thing God understands, it's sacrificing for others.

Each man should give what he has decided in his heart to
give, not reluctantly or under compulsion, for God loves a
cheerful giver. (2 Corinthians 9:7)

Here is my [Paul's] advice about what is best for you in this matter: Last year you were the first not only to give but also to have the desire to do so. Now finish the work, so that your eager willingness to do it may be matched by your completion of it, according to your means. For if the willingness is there, the gift is acceptable according to what one has, not according to what he does not have. (2 Corinthians 8:10–12)

Someone in the crowd said to him, "Teacher, tell my brother to divide the inheritance with me."

Jesus replied, "Man, who appointed me a judge or an arbiter between you?" Then he said to them, "Watch out! Be on your guard against all kinds of greed; a man's life does not consist in the abundance of his possessions."

And he told them this parable: "The ground of a certain rich man produced a good crop. He thought to himself, 'What shall I do? I have no place to store my crops.'

"Then he said, 'This is what I'll do. I will tear down my barns and build bigger ones, and there I will store all my grain and my goods. And I'll say to myself, "You have plenty of good things laid up for many years. Take life easy; eat, drink and be merry." '

"But God said to him, 'You fool! This very night your life will be demanded from you. Then who will get what you have prepared for yourself?'

"This is how it will be with anyone who stores up things for himself but is not rich toward God" (Luke 12:13–21).

Be careful not to do your "acts of righteousness" before men, to be seen by them. If you do, you will have no reward from your Father in heaven.

So when you give to the needy, do not announce it

with trumpets, as the hypocrites do in the synagogues and on the streets, to be honored by men. I tell you the truth, they have received their reward in full. But when you give to the needy, do not let your left hand know what your right hand is doing, so that your giving may be in secret. Then your Father, who sees what is done in secret, will reward you. (Matthew 6:1–4)

Do not store up for yourselves treasures on earth, where moth and rust destroy, and where thieves break in and steal. But store up for yourselves treasures in heaven, where moth and rust do not destroy, and where thieves do not break in and steal. For where your treasure is, there your heart will be also. (Matthew 6:19–21)

Woe to you who are rich, for you have already received your comfort. (Luke 6:24)

And there you have it: Our answer to every good question about Christianity that we could imagine you asking. If our imaginations didn't reach quite far enough—if you still have questions you'd like answered, issues or considerations you'd like us to address, or if the answers we gave led to other questions you'd like to ask—please don't hesitate to let us know, via our e-mail addresses below. We'd love to hear from you.

We're sad that we're done writing this book—but thrilled to think that *you,* friend, are just beginning to write the magnificent story of your personal relationship with Jesus Christ. What a story that will be! Whether you're coming into the faith for the first time or recommitting yourself to the Lord, brace yourself to be awed by the vast array of ways in which your life will begin to every day improve. Being with God makes being on earth easier, better, smoother, deeper, more rewarding, more productive, more fulfilling. It *affirms* life in a way that unless you have experienced it, you really can't imagine.

Start experiencing it! Embrace the Lord! Let him embrace you! Accept the invitation that God himself is everywhere extending to you, outside *and* inside.

Come on in, friend. The water, to say the least, is fine.

As Paul said, "There is but one God, the Father, from whom all things came and for whom we live; and there is but one Lord, Jesus Christ, through whom all things came and through whom we live" (1 Corinthians 8:6).

And there it is: Every question to every answer any one of us could ever ask.

Okay! Don't forget to write and say hi! God bless you!

Yours in the mind-boggling beneficence and endless grace of the Lord,

Steve (SArterburn@newlife.com) and John (johnshore@sbc global.net)

Free discussion guide available for download at www .bethanyhouse.com/BeingChristianDiscussionGuide

About the Authors

STEPHEN ARTERBURN is founder and chairman of New Life Ministries—the nation's largest faith-based broadcast, counseling, and treatment ministry—and host of the nationally syndicated *New Life Live!* daily radio program heard on more than 180 stations nationwide. A nationally known speaker, he has been featured on *CNN Live* and in the *New York Times, US News & World Report, Rolling Stone,* and many other media outlets.

Steve founded the Women of Faith conferences and is a best-selling author of more than seventy books, including the multi-million selling *Every Man's Battle* series and *Midlife Manual for Men.* He has been nominated for numerous writing awards and won three Gold Medallion awards for writing excellence.

Steve and his family live in Laguna Beach, California. For more information, go to *www.newlife.com.*

JOHN SHORE, an experienced writer and editor, is the author of *I'm OK—You're Not: The Message We're Sending Nonbelievers and Why We Should Stop; Penguins, Pain and the Whole Shebang;* and coauthor of *Comma Sense* and *Midlife Manual for Men.* He also blogs on *Crosswalk.com.* John and his wife live in San Diego.

Building Character and Transforming Lives Through God's Truth

New Life Ministries is a non profit organization, founded by author and speaker, Stephen Arterburn. Our mission is to identify and compassionately respond to the needs of those seeking healing and restoration through God's truth.

New Life's ministry of healing and transformation includes:

- *New Life Live!* – our daily, call-in counseling radio program hosted by Stephen Arterburn. To find a station near you call 1-800-NEW-LIFE or go to www.newlife.com. You can also listen online.
- *Counselors* – our network of over 700 counselors nationwide. Call 1-800-NEW-LIFE to find one near you.
- *Weekend Intensive Workshops and Seminars*
  - *New Life Weekend*
  - *Every Man's Battle*
- *Coaching* – Our personal coaching program is "Professional Accountability" to come alongside you and give you solution-focused direction.
- *Website*
  - Podcasts and broadcasts of *New Life Live!*
  - Blogs, message boards and chats
  - Our online store, featuring products by our radio show hosts
  - Find workshops and counselors in your area
- *24-Hour Call Center* – There is someone answering calls in our Call Center, 24 hours a day, 7 days a week, 365 days a year.

1-800-NEW-LIFE   newlife.com

NEW LIFE Weekend

with New Life host, Steve Arterburn live!

This weekend includes:

- 2-night hotel stay, including meals
- 5 sessions with Steve Arterburn live
- 1 follow-up phone coaching session
- 6 small-group counseling sessions led by a New Life Christian counselor, focusing on one of our specialty programs dealing with:

•Anger •Body Image/Weight Loss
•Creating Boundaries •Fear/Anxiety
•Forgiveness •Getting Unstuck •Marriage
•Depression and Grief •Post-Abortive Healing
•Restoring a Wife's Heart •Surviving Sexual Abuse

EVERY MAN'S BATTLE Workshop

The goal of the *Every Man's Battle* three-day workshop is to equip each man with the tools necessary to maintain sexual integrity and to enjoy healthy, productive relationships. By the completion of the program, attendees will have insight into the nature of sexual temptation and be able to use those tools to battle it.

1-800-NEW-LIFE   newlife.com